CONTENTS

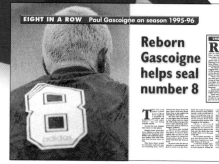

EIGHT IN A ROW Paul Gascoigne on season 1995-96

Reborn Gascoigne helps seal number 8

ONE IN A ROW Season 1988 - 89

'He had as much natural ability as anyone I've ever seen'

ALL THE STATS FROM 9 GLORIOUS YEARS

All of us who passionately support

Rangers Football Club feel an immense sense

of pride at the achievement of winning

nine league championships in a row.

David Murray

May 7, 1997

9 - Official Tribute to the League Champions 1989-97
by Iain King

Published on behalf of Rangers Football Club by First Press Publishing Limited
193-197 Bath Street, Glasgow G2 4HU

© Rangers Football Club, 1997

ISBN 1 901603 03 2

Printed and bound in Scotland

193/197 Bath Street, Glasgow, G2 4HU
Telephone: 0141 226 2200. Fax: 0141 248 1099

FOREWORD

By David E Murray
Chairman of Rangers Football Club

'We shall look back on these nine years and say this was truly the golden era of Rangers'

ALL of us who passionately support Rangers Football Club feel an immense sense of pride at the achievement of winning nine league championships in a row.

It is a particular privilege to be part of that success and to be writing the foreword to this historic book as chairman of the club.

Personally nine-in-a-row is something to be cherished because its start fortunately co-incided with my arrival at the club.

There have been other successful eras in the late 1920's and early 30s, the early 60s and late 70s. These were marvellous years to be enjoyed, but this eclipses them all.

I have to be honest and say I never fully realised the responsibility I was taking on when I came to Rangers.

But every year, with every passing championship, I have grown to learn what it all means. Perhaps I under-estimated the importance of reaching the nine. It must have been hard for a Rangers' fan during the leaner times, so this unprecedented series of victories will be relished all the more.

But it's about being able to call on the best, not just in terms of players, but in hundreds of people behind the scenes who drive Rangers forward as a thriving business every day of the week.

The generating of millions of

pounds from commercial activities to spend on new players, constantly upgrading the facilities to make a match day at Ibrox something special and exciting, a big occasion.

Ground breaking business ventures such as our new association with Scottish Television and Sky Scottish to create a special programme on our unique Jumbotronic screens with the ability to beam matches direct back to the ground.

On July 5, 1997 we will launch our new Nike strip and training wear. I would truly appreciate every true Rangers fan buying goods DIRECT from the club.

Buying goods DIRECT from Rangers can be your way of making an additional significant contribution. This is an area in which we can collectively give the club a major financial boost.

The new partnership with Nike proves we don't just talk about these deals – we deliver them.

And as long as I am chairman I can promise everyone who believes in Rangers that I will not settle for anything but the best. No effort will be spared in delivering further success to make the club even greater, setting new targets for ourselves, working to take the club to the next level.

There have been many highs and lows in these last nine years. I have been fortunate that every year under my stewardship we have won the league. But equally each season has always thrown up the unexpected situation.

I will never forget the back to back defeats we had at Celtic in 1991 because I have always felt that they had such a huge effect on

Graeme Souness. We had three players sent off in one of those games and inwardly I think it may have been the time he genuinely felt it was time to move and consequently he was approached by Liverpool.

Graeme's involvement at Rangers brought me into this great club so when he left to join in 1991 it was a bitter disappointment.

He genuinely felt that at times the authorities were trying to make him work with his hands tied. He told me I should go too before it got any worse – but I was always a long-term player not someone for just the short term.

To me a challenge or a crisis was something to be dealt with head-on. I've coped with such situations all my life. Leaving was simply not an option.

Graeme's aggressive style

turned the club round and restored our pride. His name had assisted in bringing great international players like Butcher, Woods, Steven, Gough and Hateley to play alongside the home grown Scots like McCoist, Durrant and then Ferguson who were so vital in taking the club to new heights.

All this helped lay the foundation for the nine successive championships and Graeme was a vital ingredient at that time.

But the club has become big enough on its own reputation to attract the top players. In retrospect I think Graeme going helped the club move to the next phase of development.

From then on it has been the style and dedication of Walter Smith which has taken the club to the next stage.

I have the utmost respect

for Walter as a manager and even more so as a man. Above all he epitomises the dignity of the club.

He conducts himself at all times in an exemplary fashion under a pressure which would crush most other people. He has given the club the most loyal of service and deserves the praise and rewards he justly receives.

He is a football man. The man who Jock Stein, Alex Ferguson, Jim McLean and Graeme wanted at their right hand.

No-one has ever served a better apprenticeship for the job of Rangers manager than Walter. He is the equal of anyone who has ever held the job.

He motivates the players game in, game out in our league and we haven't slipped up once in nine years. The only thing he has

not delivered yet is a European trophy. If he was able to do that within the next few years then he would be the greatest Rangers' manager EVER.

Europe means a lot to me – and it has had more than its fair share of lows. But I don't believe that any other big club in that arena has had to survive with the additional pressure of achieving a domestic record like nine-in-a-row.

Leeds United home and away, then coming back to win 1-0 away on the Saturday when we played below our best – but full of Rangers character – were very special. The fight back against Marseille at Ibrox, Gascoigne's hat-trick to secure our eighth consecutive title and Hateley's league-clinching double in 1991 were all special occasions. These were great

games which will live with me forever.

In those big European nights I think we all felt part of the passion, the big occasion – a feeling of 'that's where the club belongs'. The team playing at its peak on the big football stage.

So now we have made another major piece of history. I said at the club's AGM this year that if we could get through this season and win it then a major weight would be lifted from our shoulders.

Nine-in-a-row has brought so much pressure not only to Rangers. When you are second you are branded a failure.

Now we must look to a wider future. Many clubs are at the end of rebuilding their grounds and I have a real hope that we can expand the game as a whole within Scotland.

For now though, let's celebrate the public acknowledgement that we are winners and in quieter moments too. I rarely go to the celebrations. I come away quietly and don't like to look for the plaudits.

I come home and sit in my house in Edinburgh, go out for a meal with family and friends and think I've done my job. I'm happy. It's then I can indulge myself and look back fondly on it all.

People like to reminisce about Ritchie, Shearer and Caldow but I think years from now they will reminisce about Goram, Gough and Laudrup.

I believe then we shall look back on the last nine years and say that THIS was truly the golden era of the club.

David E Murray,
Chairman
Rangers Football Club

This chapter is brought to you
in association with

ROCK
STEADY

SECURITY
LTD

Seething Souness starts the ball rolling

GRAEME SOUNESS had ridden on the crest of a wave since sweeping into Ibrox as the saviour of Rangers in 1986. Two years later, he was in danger of drowning.

In their centenary year, Celtic had drawn on a reservoir of emotion to surge to a league and Cup double under the leadership of Lisbon Lion Billy McNeill.

Souness, meanwhile, faced a crisis – fans' favourite and stand-in skipper Graham Roberts was axed after a bitter dressing-room bust-up with his boss following a final day defeat by Aberdeen.

Danish international left-back Jan Bartam had also clashed with the manager and fled to Denmark to slaughter Souness in the Press in his homeland.

But the former Liverpool and Scotland captain faced the daunting challenge the way he'd tackled every other threat in his path to the top. He stared it down.

Souness knew he had to come up with the solution and £2million was shelled out on two players who would become part of the heart of nine-in-a-row.

Rangers-daft Ian Ferguson achieved a lifetime ambition at the age of just 20 when Souness finally got his man at the fourth time of asking for a cool £1million.

He'd cost St Mirren just £60,000 from Clyde two seasons earlier but the Rangers manager believed he had the perfect modern-day midfielder.

Nine years later Ferguson – although plagued by injury and

illness throughout his Ibrox career – was one of just three players, alongside Richard Gough and Ally McCoist, who could claim medals from all nine title triumphs.

Everton right-back Gary Stevens matched that Fergie price tag and was to play 107 league games in six glorious years for the club before departing for Tranmere Rovers. The Ferguson signing was Souness' 20th in two years in the Ibrox hotseat and brought his spending to £6.7m.

He'd failed in an audacious bid to land Ian Rush, bound for a Liverpool return, from Juventus but he recalled: "I had to act because we'd had problems the year before - it was my toughest time as Rangers manager.

"And it was all down to one

CHAPTER 1

GRAEME SOUNESS looked round the Ibrox dressing-room as a season that yielded only the Skol Cup drew to a close in May 1988 and stared at his dejected players.

"So you're content, are you?" he asked "Happy to win the title then give it to Celtic the next season. Is that the way it's going to be?" Searching questions, and, within 12 months, he had the answers as Rangers lifted the Skol Cup once more, won the title and just failed to lift the Treble in a Scottish Cup Final defeat from their Old Firm foes.

German cracks Cologne ended the UEFA Cup campaign early but on the domestic scene Rangers were once more kings.

Souness' signings Ian Ferguson, John Brown, Gary Stevens and Kevin Drinkell were a huge success in their first full seasons and it was to be the first step on the way to nine-in-a-row.

'The fans didn't have a whiff of what was to come'

thing – Terry Butcher broke his leg.

"In my time at Rangers, there were no bigger influences in the dressing-room than Terry and Ray Wilkins.

"I saw something of the same kind of quality in Richard Gough and he went on to be the rock that nine-in-a-row was built on."

The first test of Souness' big bucks new-look side came in the less than salubrious surroundings of Douglas Park against Hamilton Accies on August 13.

Stevens got off to a flyer with a thumping shot for the first.

A predatory diving header from Ally McCoist, after some magic on the wing from Mark Walters, sealed it.

Souness said: "A lot of people baulked at the £1m I paid for Gary – they said it was too much for a right-back.

"But I knew what I was getting. He had some weaknesses going forward but he was a superb defender. There were few better.

"He had pace and when he came to the club I could set up game plans safe in the knowledge that no-one was going to harm us down the right."

A barren 0-0 draw with Hibs followed, though, and the fans did not even have a whiff of what was to come in the first Old Firm game of the campaign at Ibrox.

At the age of

35, Souness was to be troubled by a calf injury throughout that season and only made six league appearances as a sub.

But, fittingly for the man who'd given the club their pride back, one of them came as Rangers recorded their biggest league win over Celtic in 29 years.

RANGERS were to triumph 5-1 yet within five minutes they were behind when Frank McAvennie snapped up a half-chance.

The fusillade that followed shot forlorn keeper Ian Andrews' Celtic career to pieces.

McCoist swept home a quickfire equaliser then Wilkins produced one of the most memorable volleys to grace Ibrox – and as TV commentator Jock Brown hollered above the bedlam, it really was a goal 'Made in England'.

Stevens' throw was nodded on by Butcher and knocked out by Paul McStay to Wilkins. Razor's technique, as ever, was perfect and the sweetly struck shot tore away from the bewildered Hoops keeper.

Andrews made a horrific blunder to palm home a McCoist looping header after the break and strikes from another Souness acquisition, Kevin Drinkell, and Mark Walters finished the game off.

Even the player-manager was left breathless by it all and smiled: "I'll never forget that day against Celtic.

"We beat our bitterest rivals 5-1 and the punters went home disappointed because we'd stopped scoring with 27 minutes left!

"I did feel a little sorry for poor Ian Andrews in their goal but 5-1 was kind to them."

Ian Durrant then scored and inspired a 2-0 win at Motherwell before Walters' goal gave the team an edgy

COUNTDOWN TO DISASTER... *Durrant tracks Simpson before the tackle which nearly ended the Ibrox star's career*

'Disaster was to strike in a frenetic match'

1-0 UEFA Cup first leg win over Katowice of Poland at Ibrox.

It was a night of frustration with play-acting Polish stars falling like extras in *Casualty* at the slightest brush with an Ibrox jersey.

In the midst of it all, the combative John Brown earned the most bizarre booking of his career.

Fed-up with a constant series of stoppages, Brown dumped the Polish trainer's hefty medical bag onto the track only to see it burst open, sending bandages and sprays careering down the running track.

The bewildered ref booked a red-faced Bomber for tackling the red-cross chest from behind.

Souness grinned: "That summed him up, that level of commitment. I'd come up against John Brown at Dundee when I was still playing.

"It was a cold, frosty night and the surface meant that tackles were flying.

"I gave him a couple of dabs and he just hit me back harder. I thought 'You'll do for me' "

At £350,000 Brown, now a coach at Ibrox and still registered as a player, was to prove one of the shrewdest signings of a manager so often painted simply as Mr Moneybags.

It's too easily forgotten, the wisdom that Souness often used in getting the most out of assets and then selling them on for a profit.

Brown, though, never wanted to go anywhere because like Ferguson he was living his dream.

And Souness revealed:

"Even the signing had its problems because he was such a Rangers fanatic.

"He was convinced the phone call when I got in touch was a wind-up, that it just couldn't be true he was coming to Ibrox!"

DURRANT'S form, meanwhile, was scaling the peaks. At the age of just 21, he had it all — poise, balance, passing and the vision to sear in to the box beyond his strikers. Defences found his runs impossible to track.

He had the hallmarks of the complete midfielder but time was ticking away on all his promise.

At Tynecastle on September 17 he drove in to the box to be felled by Neil Berry before dusting himself down and rifling the spot-kick home.

Sub Scott Nisbet tied up a 2-1 win despite skipper Butcher's first goal of the season – at the wrong end.

The Souness revolution may have come a little too late to catch Davie Cooper in his prime, but he still had a part to play.

The winger was the force behind a 2-1 Ibrox win over St Mirren. Coop scored from the spot and set up Walters for the headed back post winner after ex-Ibrox star Billy Davies put the Buddies ahead.

And it was the Moody Blue's introduction as a sub at Tannadice three days later that brought the cross

for Ferguson to secure the points. Rangers were on a roll now and a 2-0 win over Dundee left them clear at the top. They had dropped just one point in their first eight games.

And the success story continued in Europe as they stormed into the Poles in Katowice in a 4-2 win that featured a double from Butcher and goals from the in-form Durrant and Ferguson.

Souness knew he had a precious talent in his midfield – on October 8 at Pittodrie, that talent was savagely left in tatters.

Just ten days after signing from Aston Villa, Neale Cooper rifled Rangers in front, but, in the midst of a frenetic match, disaster was to strike. As play raged in a series of fiery exchanges,

Neil Simpson flew into a fury and smashed his studs into Durrant's knee. It was a sickening challenge.

Durrant's cruciate ligament and his career were left hanging by a thread.

He was to come back two-and-a-half years later but would never again be the same thrilling player he had been.

Yet Souness believes his former star could have dodged that appalling tackle if he'd been more streetwise in the line of fire.

He insisted: "It still hurts me yet when I think back to that day because he only had himself to blame – he went to sleep.

"He played the ball and then he looked away and he got caught so very badly.

"Football was so easy for

him but if he had been a little brighter upstairs that day he would have avoided it.

"He came back bravely and he's still been a very good Rangers servant.

"But the truth is he could have achieved so much more."

Souness had survived on the battlegrounds of England and Europe, fighting for the right to play Liverpool's winning brand of football with the arrogant swagger that became his trademark.

From Wales' Peter Nicholas to Iceland's Siggi Jonsson and a red card for poleaxing Hibs star George McCluskey on his Premier League debut, he had left his mark in some infamous encounters.

The player-manager knew

'He had as much natural ability as anyone I've ever seen'

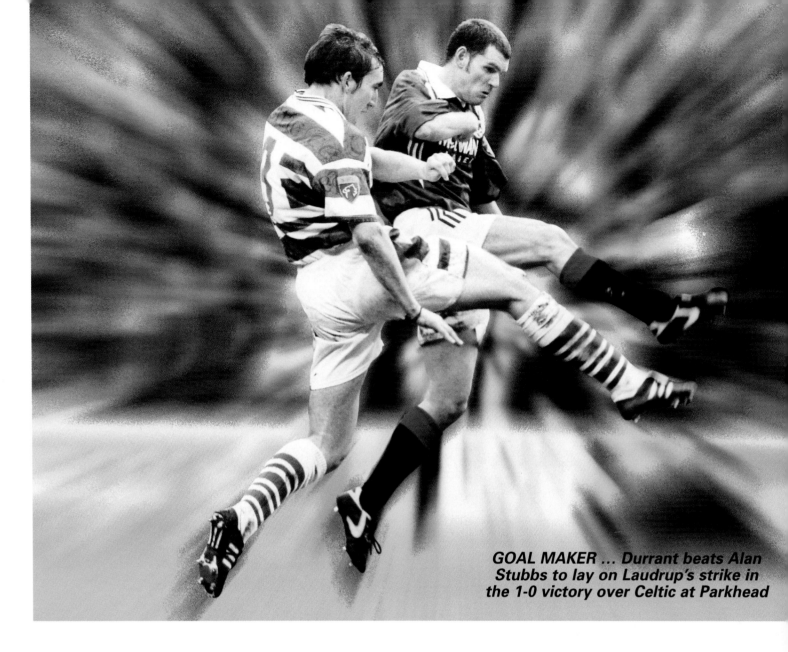

GOAL MAKER ... Durrant beats Alan Stubbs to lay on Laudrup's strike in the 1-0 victory over Celtic at Parkhead

where to look for ambushes but in his naivete, Durrant, in the ferocious passage of a tension-packed game, simply didn't see it coming.

To this day, Souness feels guilty that he wasn't on the pitch as his minder.

He revealed: "There is one other thing that has always nagged at me about that day – I was not there to protect him.

"Okay, I was 35 then, but I could still do a job and I had played as a sub a few times that season.

"But I wasn't stripped that day at Pittodrie and I watched him go down.

"I could have been on there sorting the other guy out and keeping him away from Durranty.

"It cut me to the quick to lose him. He had as much natural ability as anyone I have ever seen.

"I said he could have made

it in Italy and I would stick by that."

Nine years on from that fateful game, it was fitting that on the day nine-in-a-row was all but clinched with a 1-0 triumph at Parkhead, it should be Durrant who beat Alan Stubbs to loft the ball goalward for the winner.

The official scoresheet credited Brian Laudrup with the goal, but, in the hearts of the fans, the strike will forever belong to the midfielder who means so much to them after all he has come through.

Lying on a table in the Ibrox massage room, as his battered leg received the treatment to prepare him

for another outing in his beloved light blue, Durrant challenges McCoist for the title as king of the one-liners.

But his face was a mask of disillusionment when he recalled the day that saw him scythed down while at the height of his powers.

And he confessed: "It angers me still because I was flying back then. I like to think I could have gone on to fulfil Graeme's prediction that I could have made it in Italy but I never got the chance.

"I have always loved playing for Rangers in Europe but a move to the continent never materialised for me."

Durrant listened to all the stick heaped on Souness

when he quit Gers for Liverpool in April 1991 and shook his head in disbelief.

He knew the debt the club owed him.

He said: "Graeme Souness took a lot of time out to talk to me about football and he was one of the BEST things that ever happened to me at Rangers.

"Sure, he would chin you if you'd stepped out of line off the park but once you were on the football park it was back to business.

"For myself he laid the foundations for the Rangers of today because when he arrived the club was going nowhere.

"He brought the good days back. People think the injury was the toughest spell for me and, yes, that was very hard.

"But I also remember when I was breaking through there would be 6000 in Ibrox and the team

LEGEND THAT NEVER WAS … *Derek Ferguson could have been a Rangers great but his relationship with Souness turned sour*

Souness was a hard man but that was never me

was losing. It was a truly magnificent stadium yet it was ghostly and you could hear every shout of abuse."

For Durrant there was a long and lonely fight ahead and spells of deep depression when he admits he felt like quitting football.

But, from somewhere, he found the spirit to go on as his team-mates stayed on track for the title.

Close pal McCoist tapped into his resources of bravery at Easter Road four days later as he ignored six stitches in a head wound to nod home the clincher.

With the Skol Cup Final against old foes Aberdeen looming, Souness was then hit by a transfer request from a player he had treasured when he first arrived at the club.

On October 26, 1986, two Rangers fans arrived as Ibrox idols as they starred in a 2-1 Skol Cup Final win over Celtic.

Souness would go on to name Derek Ferguson as the best young midfield player he had ever seen and also hand Durrant that weighty assessment of his worth.

Yet in 1997, we can look back and see that they can claim just 13 international caps between them.

As Durrant flourished back then, Ferguson was out of favour and, at the age of 21, wanted out of Ibrox.

Souness rated Derek far better than he himself had been as a youngster but the first demand for a move was the signal of the beginning of the end of a player who should have been a Rangers great.

The rift was eventually healed when Ferguson returned to the team a month later and he played a significant role that season.

But the following two seasons brought just nine league games and he was allowed to leave for Hearts in a £750,000 move.

To this day the relationship with Souness that turned sour still rankles.

Derek said: "I've always felt it was unfair of him to come away with remarks like that when I was only a kid.

"He'd done it all yet he compared me to him. Souness was a hard

man and that was never me. I was never a clone of him and I was stubborn when we had arguments.

"I should have shut my mouth but I would answer him back and barge into his office and demand to talk to him."

There was only going to be one winner and without Ferguson, single-minded Souness turned his attention to the first silverware of the season, up for grabs in

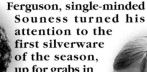

KOP MATES … Souness and Kenny Dalglish renew their Liverpool partnership

a Skol Final that was a re-run of the classic clash with Aberdeen a year earlier.

They said the 3-3 draw in 1987, before Rangers won 5-3 on penalties, could never be matched.

In front of 72,122 frenzied fans, however, the teams came pretty close.

The venue was the old Hampden Park, and Aberdeen lost a farcical opener.

David Robertson, who would become a critical part of Walter Smith's Rangers, was short with a throw-in to Theo Snelders and the wily Kevin Drinkell nipped in.

Drinkell may have learned his football on the less than glamorous stages of Grimsby and Norwich but he had savvy to spare.

As the ball squirmed free, he smuggled his way to just inside the box and waited for Snelders' inevitable challenge.

Referee George Smith pointed to the spot and goal grabber McCoist was coolness personified.

Just 15 days after the Durrant storm, it was a powderkeg occasion, but this time the fuse was lit for the right reasons and the goals flew in.

Davie Dodds, now first team coach at Rangers, bit the hand that was to feed him when he guided home the equaliser with his knee.

But Ian Ferguson responded with a ripping scissors kick before Dodds once more levelled it at 2-2 with a looping header over the stranded Chris Woods from Jim Bett's cross.

The nerves were then shredded in an incredible closing two minutes after Bett missed a sitter when he strode clean through.

A typical McCoist six-yard swoop on a deflection from Willie Miller saw him volley home after Gough put the ball back in the mixer from a Walters' corner.

That made it 3-2 to Souness' side and there was still time for an appalling misjudgment from Butcher to give Dodds sight of goal four yards out but Stevens somehow kept it out and the Skol Cup was destined for the glittering Ibrox trophy room once more.

Six days later it was a jaded Rangers side which went to Love Street and only a late header from short-term signing Andy Gray – a veteran at last playing for his boyhood heroes – salvaged a 1-1 draw with St Mirren.

At the start of the season Souness had promised that he would play only in emergencies, but now Durrant and team-mate John McGregor were counted out

MAIN MAN … even stars such as 007 Sean Connery (inset) regard David Murray as a business genius

'Murray pulled off the biggest cash coup of his life'

for the rest of the campaign.

The manager sought a cure for his long-term calf trouble and Dutch physio Hans Diest put him through a tortuous three weeks of treatment in a bid to find a cure.

It didn't work – and the man so often clad in the best Armani off the pitch could never really put on his working clothes with conviction again.

Hearts were routinely disposed of 3-0 before the patience that Souness had instilled in Rangers paid off in a home clash with Motherwell.

The game was all square at 1-1 with 90 minutes gone.

Deep into stoppage time, the recalled Derek Ferguson threw his markers a dummy and found Brown.

Bomber's cross was flicked on by Ian Ferguson and there was Drinkell leaping at the back post to plant a header past the despairing Cammy Duncan.

It was the type of late show that so often secures the Championship.

There was a setback, though, in a 3-1 defeat at Parkhead before Hamilton were seen off and the side stumbled to a 0-0 draw at Dundee.

Away from the action, the stakes were beginning to rise. Souness was pour-

ing his body and soul into the club and on November 24 he rocked Rangers to the core once more.

The manager's close friend, David Murray, at 37 a self-made multi-millionaire from deals in metals and property, pulled off the financial coup of his life to take control of the biggest club in Scotland.

His business genius meant the acquisition of a £22million-rated asset was done with one flourish of

MY PLEDGE TO RANGERS
Murray spells out future at Ibrox
SHAUN IS TOP OF THE LOT

his pen for just £6 million.

It marked the dawn of a new era for Rangers as American-based recluse Lawrence Marlborough, boss of the Lawrence building empire, ended his family's 25-year reign over the club.

Souness also ploughed in £600,000 of his own cash to become a director of the club with a 10 per cent share.

He felt then that he had a "lifetime" stake but, two-and-a-half years later, he

23

would walk out the door for Liverpool, close to tears.

Once more the man who left Anfield to conquer Italian football with Sampdoria was ruled by the ceaseless ambition which has been his master.

Souness quit and he advised his chairman to do the same. But Murray was made of stronger stuff. It made him even more determined to bring unparralleled success to the club. Rangers and Scottish football would never be the same again.

But that was still for the future. The Murray/Souness partnership got off to a flyer at home to Aberdeen with Gough drilling home a left-foot drive to seal a crucial win.

Defeats from Dundee United and Hearts were tough to take and as his obsession with Rangers drove him on Souness had problems on and off the field.

Wife Danielle had flown home to Majorca with his three children and his eight-year marriage was on the rocks. The pressure on him was mounting.

But deep down he felt he was on the threshold of football history. When we spoke about those chaotic days Souness, a far mellower version these days, was ready for the fight to keep new club Southampton in the Premiership.

But the thrilling quest that drove the two friends

almost a decade ago remains fresh in his mind.

And he said: "We saw each other socially most nights and the talk was always Rangers.

"When David Murray came to the club I felt we had the greatest chance Rangers would have in their history.

"We sat at dinner one night and I told him 'This club has the chance to dominate Celtic as they have never been dominated before'.

"He always vowed to match any ambitions I had for the club and I felt I spent his money well."

Back on the field Ian McCall's sole league goal for Rangers was one to remember, an exquisite curler from the angle of the box that sealed a 1-0 win and left the Hibs keeper helpless.

Andy Goram clutching air would not be a common sight at Ibrox in the years to come.

Hamilton No.1 Alan Rough then obligingly stood rooted to the spot and watched sub Derek Ferguson's left-foot shot drift past him in a Douglas Park battle as Rangers marched out of 1988 two points clear of Dundee United.

The New Year Old Firm clash was vital but within 60 seconds Gers were behind to a Chris Morris free-kick.

Souness' side, though, simply refused to panic and after skipper Butcher headed an equaliser the streetwise Drinkell conned perennial

fall-guy Anton Rogan into another reckless challenge.

Walters smacked home the penalty, Ian Ferguson saw a shot deflected home and after a second-half bout of Celtic pressure wing king Mark sped on to a stunning ball from Derek Ferguson to wrap it up.

In the two home games with Celtic a disbelieving Ibrox crowd had watched NINE goals whistle past their vowed enemies.

They were in heaven and Souness recalled: "We were learning all the time, playing the way I wanted.

"We could absorb so much pressure and then hammer teams.

"The team was built like that and when we hit them on the break that day Walters had the pace and the finishing to make them pay."

Defeat at Motherwell the following week had Souness in a fury but the players answered his criticism in fine style at Pittodrie on January 14.

Young Derek Ferguson's uneasy truce with the manager was holding and he was enormously influential in a 2-1 win.

His header rolled home off Stuart Munro's thigh for a scrambled first but the second was born of the sort of pass midfielders see in their dreams.

It came from Ian Ferguson as he sliced the Dons apart with an instant volleyed ball over the top that sprang their offside trap, and Derek raced clear to do the rest.

After 13 matches and

three months out with a torn hamstring Rangers welcomed back McCoist for the home clash with Dundee and, naturally, he scored in a 3-1 success.

But at Tannadice on February 11 all hell broke loose for Souness after Stuart Munro fired his side in front.

A hopeful punt into the box three minutes into injury time careered off the shoulder of Gary Stevens and into goal handing United a 1-1 draw.

The Rangers manager was furious and clashes with a linesman led to a £100 fine and an SFA ban from the touchline for the rest of the season.

It was to be another two successful but often strife-torn years until Souness walked out on Rangers but the seeds were sown here.

Banished from the touchline he was to be caught up in frustration and rage when his portable phone link to the bench packed up during a toiling display in a 0-0 Scottish Cup semi-final draw with St Johnstone two months later.

He ran down to the dugout twice to pass on instructions to No.2 Walter Smith under the noses of the then SFA top brass of president David Will and secretary Ernie Walker. They hammered him.

On April 27 – two days before his team clinched the title – Graeme Souness was fined £2,000 and banned from the touchline until the end of the NEXT season.

He would now not be

'All hell broke loose at Tannadice'

allowed in the dugout until August 1990 and to make matters worse, assistant Smith joined him in the stand after he too was hit with a year's ban for a bust-up with a linesman.

Souness recalled: "There was so much going against me back then.

"I was banned from the touchline and I felt as if the SFA were STRANGLING me.

"I was being followed by the media in my private life and there were days when they had helicopters flying over my house.

"I had a lot of personal problems and I was putting myself under huge pressure to make Rangers bigger and

better. I felt as if I should adopt the Rangers song 'No one likes us, we don't care' scratch that ... I felt it had been written by me."

The manager may have been under increasing strain but after that clash with United the players had produced wins over St Mirren, Hamilton – a match that featured a scoring debut for Mel Sterland – and Hibs.

And at Parkhead on April 1 they turned in a belligerent performance the boss could be proud of to notch up their first win in the east end of Glasgow for nine years. Wilkins' centre found

ALLY OOPS ... McCoist claims the goal against Celtic that really belongs to Ian Ferguson

'My bust-up with a tea lady was the last straw'

Drinkell to direct home a header that flicked in off Steve McCahill and then Ian Ferguson's ferocious free-kick knocked Packie Bonner off his feet for the second.

McCoist followed the keeper's parry into the net and claimed it.

The official league handbook for that year actually gives it to the shameless striker in an act of larceny. It was Ferguson's goal.

Andy Walker pulled one back but after all the controversy of a year fuelled by flare-ups Souness was on the title home straight. And if April was marred by those shock bans for the management team, on the field it was business as usual.

McCoist grabbed the points against Motherwell before sealing it at St Mirren after Ian Ferguson had

screamed a scorching shot into the top corner against his old club.

Party time came on April 29 against Hearts with Sterland dominating the celebrations after two first half goals.

Drinkell – the club's top league scorer that season – then half-volleyed home a belter before striding on to Tom Cowan's clever pass to make it 4-0.

Sterland was the hero of the hour, yet Souness reflected: "I spent £800,000 on Mel but I got the money back when I sold him in the close season.

"At Rangers with a big bankroll you could afford quick fixes like that.

"But what I would do is make sure buys such as that came from England because I could then get the money back when I sold them back down south.

"I'd never have gambled

cash like that on a short-term eastern European, for instance, because if they flop you are stuck with them."

That type of acumen had served Souness so well.

And after a Tayside double over Dundee and United – when he first cheekily defied his ban to sit on the bench as a sub – he was delighted to see another signing, £1million Richard Gough, named the Scottish Football Writers' Association Player of the Year.

He recalled: "Richard had first struck me as a very special type during 1986 World Cup in Mexico.

"He's a model athlete who looks after his fitness and had all the skills required for the modern game.

"He cost me a few quid more than I had bargained for but

I didn't regret a penny of it."

The Cup Final defeat from Celtic when Gary Stevens' blunder handed the winner to Joe Miller was a sad end to Souness' season. And he insisted his appearance as a sub for the last 32 minutes was his last bow as player – a promise the showman in him couldn't quite stick to.

Two years later it was over, the Souness revolution ended with the famed hard man close to breaking down as he left for Liverpool.

Six weeks before he decided to go he had had a bizarre bust-up with St Johnstone tea lady Aggie Moffat after she accused the manager of leaving the visitors' dressing room in a mess.

The row raged on outside the boardroom until Saints chairman Geoff Brown intervened and Souness sighed: "Everywhere I turned I felt obstructed down to

ALL OVER ... Murray listens grim-faced as Souness announces his departure

stupid bust-ups with people like that tea lady at St Johnstone, it was ridiculous.

"That was one of the final straws to be honest, I just wondered what the point was.

"The aggravation was mounting and I was sick of it."

Yet after all the pressure and all the strain any other club in the world could have offered Graeme Souness the keys to the manager's office and he'd have said: "No thanks."

He insisted: "Liverpool were the ONLY club I would have left Rangers for and they asked twice and I knocked them back twice.

"Then they asked a third time and I succumbed, the lure was too much.

"It was very emotional when I told David, we'd been friends for a long time by then.

"He told me I was making the biggest blunder of my life and football-wise he was RIGHT.

"When I decided to go I told David: "Walter's your man, no mistake."

"I knew he wanted a big name but I told him he had the right candidate on his doorstep.

"Walter had been a great No.2, the steadying influence when I was flying off the handle."

Who knows what toll his role as the man who awoke the sleeping giant of

Rangers took on Graeme Souness? It certainly cost him his first marriage and in May 1992 he was a pale, gaunt and drawn figure on the Wembley turf clutching the FA Cup. He was recovering from triple heart bypass surgery but wanted to be there when his Liverpool side triumphed over Sunderland.

Yet a driven winner's outlook on life had been changed forever and he has certainly mellowed since the end of his Kop reign, marriage to second wife Karen and a spell at Turkish side Galatasary before the switch to Southampton.

He remains philosophical about his fate since he walked out the Ibrox exit door and he said: "The biggest problem I had with my heart was the genes I inherited, it's in my family.

"But there's no doubt that the stress and strain I put myself through at Ibrox helped put me in a hospital bed.

"I will always accept that David said I made the biggest mistake of my life going but you cannot have everything in this world.

"If I had not moved I would not have met Karen who has been the best thing that's happened to me.

"And I'm happier now than I've ever been in my life, you can't put a price on that."

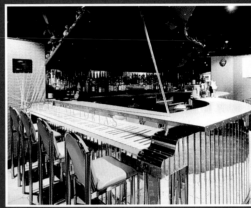

ARE YOU READY ?

On the 5th July Rangers will launch the all new Nike strip
and range of football, leisure wear and accessories.

UPPORT YOUR CLUB AND SHARE IN OUR FUTURE SUCCESS

By purchasing the new Nike range directly from the Rangers shops
or Rangers mail order you are making a real and significant contribution
to the finances, fortunes and future of the club.

We'll reinvest the profits in players - other retailers don't!

Buy direct and support your club

NEW HOTLINE NUMBER 0990 99 1997

This chapter is brought to you
in association with

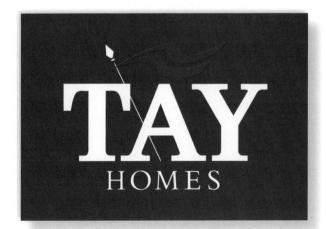

CHAPTER 2

GRAEME SOUNESS' trademark icy glare defiantly met a packed Ibrox Press conference before a grin creased the tanned, craggy features – he'd just pulled off the bravest Old Firm transfer heist in history.

Former Celtic idol Maurice Johnston was a Gers player and July 12, 1989, will be remembered as the day Souness and chairman David Murray began to shape the new Rangers.

A storm of controversy and criticism greeted Johnston's arrival from French side Nantes amid predictions that there would be swathes of empty seats as sup-porters protested against the sign-ing of a high-profile Catholic.

The inevitable furore fizzled out though and, by the end of the season, Super Mo was a hero. He became the club's top league scor-er with 15 goals and he struck twice against Celtic to play a key role in retaining the Premier crown.

An early Euro KO at the hands of Bayern Munich, Skol Cup Final defeat by Aberdeen and a Scottish Cup loss against Celtic were bitter pills to swallow – but Terry Butcher's men dug deep into their resources and roared to glory seven points clear of Aberdeen and Hearts.

Johnston heralds new era at Ibrox

TWO GAMES, no wins, no points, no goals and bottom of the league. After seven days of their title defence, the champs were finding life hard. Rangers players always know that the passion and intensity surrounding the club can quickly send them tumbling from the peaks of delight into the troughs of despair.

Losing twice on the trot is regarded as a blip at most other clubs. At Ibrox it's a crisis.

Rangers skipper Terry Butcher will never forget that awful opening in 1989 when his side were under the cosh right from the season's first whistle – and a curtain-raising 1-0 home defeat by St Mirren.

He sighed: "We unfurled the flag that day at Ibrox and the party went downhill

MAGIC MO-MENTS...Johnston powers home a double dose of trouble for Celts in the 1989/90 Old Firm Ibrox clashes

'We felt Mo was one of us now'

fast after that. Chris Woods dislocated his shoulder in a challenge with Kenny McDowall and he bundled the ball in to rub salt in the wound for us.

"Our keeper was out and we knew we were going to Easter Road – traditionally a graveyard for us – in the next game."

Hibs had haunted Gers in Edinburgh in the past and they were dead and buried again as hastily-signed Israeli keeper Bonni Ginzburg's (pictured right) league debut rapidly turned into an afternoon he'd rather forget.

Goals from Keith Houchen and Mickey Weir

left Gers on the ropes following a 2-0 defeat and, with Celtic winning both their opening fixtures, the flak was flying as the Light Blues title charge failed to get out of first gear.

August 26, the day of the season's first Old Firm clash, dawned with the daunting possibility of Graeme Souness' side lurching six points behind their bitterest rivals.

Seldom can this footballing Clash of the Titans have been so highly-charged as Johnston walked into the lions' den, wearing the blue of Rangers against the fans who had once idolised him.

Butcher recalled: "You could almost touch the tension. I have never heard anyone take so much abuse as Mo suffered that day. The Celtic fans slaughtered him mercilessly from the first second to the last.

"He missed a couple of good chances but, as far as we were concerned, he was one

of us now and we rallied round him."

After all their woes Rangers looked for inspiration in the cauldron of Celtic Park.

They found it in a captain who remains one of the club's favourite sons.

Only five minutes had passed when Trevor Steven

swung over a corner and big Tel rose above them all to thunder in a header that rocketed beyond the helpless Pat Bonner.

A huge weight had been lifted from the shoulders of the fraught champions and, although Polish striker Jacki Dziekanowski scrambled home an equaliser, Butcher maintained: "That was a huge psychological boost for us.

"To come away with a point lifted us all after that appalling start."

Despite the blunders in front of goal, Johnston had survived his first ordeal against the club he snubbed

for Ibrox. Mo never looked back.

On September 9, Graeme Souness' men played hosts to Aberdeen and Johnston leapt above the Aberdeen defence to power home a Steven cross. His first goal was to secure a crucial 1-0 win.

Johnston had been mixing with the elite at French cracks Nantes – players like Belgian midfielder Frankie Vercauteren and Argentina's Jorge Burruchaga, who scored the winner in the 1986 World Cup Final win over West Germany.

A bewildering bicycle

'Mo's season was spiced with strikes that mattered'

A KISS FOR THE KIT MAN... Jimmy Bell used to give Ally McCoist a stylish wake-up call

kick against Cyprus at Hampden which helped Scotland to a 2-1 win and took them a huge step nearer Italia 90 had been the conclusive evidence that this was a striker transformed.

Rangers were to reap the rewards and that landmark goal against the Dons set a telling pattern.

That season wasn't peppered with Mo scoring the fourth in another Ibrox romp, it was spiced with goals that mattered, strikes that won games and plundered points.

And team-mate Terry said: "The Scottish players had been stunned by his signing but he was accepted readily at the pre-season training camp in Italy.

"Personally, I was delighted because I knew he was a major player and I felt we'd kicked Celtic where it really hurt."

Johnston, though, didn't receive any special treatment from his team-mates.

In fact, when he arrived at the Gers' summer headquarters at Il Ciocco in the Tuscany hills, he found a table set separately for him with just bread and water for his evening meal!

BUTCHER said: "He also suffered at the hands of Jimmy Bell, the kitman. Ally McCoist would wake up every morning to find his training kit neatly laid outside his hotel bedroom door.

"Mo, meanwhile, had to trail all the way down to the laundry room to pick up his.

"And when the chocolate bars were being handed round after training, we

KEEPING A BUTCHER'S... Tel watches as Mike Galloway and goalscorer Nigel Spackman get to grips in the Ne'erday Old Firm clash

were all scoffing away while Johnston pleaded to be given one!"

Yet Mo has never been short of a word or 20 and he emerged unscathed from all the dressing-room baiting to forge a formidable striking partnership with close friend McCoist.

After that Aberdeen win, though, Souness' side still couldn't slot into top gear and they surrendered points in draws with Dundee and Dunfermline before Mo struck again to topple Hearts at home.

It remains one of the saddest Ibrox ironies that the Rangers Revolution came too late for two of the most gifted players ever to tug that famous light blue jersey over their heads.

Bobby Russell and the late, great Davie Cooper were tailor-made for the thinking man's football Souness brought to the club when he burst onto the Scottish scene from Sampdoria.

But they were heading into their 30s and had both past their peak when he arrived, although both later became bargain buys for the shrewd Tommy McLean at Motherwell.

October 3 gave them the chance to show that while the legs will eventually betray you, that elusive ability to see openings others can't lives on.

They passed and probed, teased and tormented and Russell scored to send his old club spiralling to a costly 1-0 Fir Park defeat.

Now Rangers were under siege to find answers to a faltering challenge – and they found it at the Ally-Mo.

McCoist and Johnston hit a golden seam of form, sharing seven goals as Dundee United, St Mirren and Hibs were dumped before an Old Firm game that will forever be etched into the memories of those who were there.

The date: November 4, 1989. The venue: A packed Ibrox. The hero: Who else but Maurice Johnston?

Time ticked away and the game seemed set to fizzle out into a goal-less draw, until Gary Stevens fired in a 88th minute cross from the right and Chris Morris fatally miscued his clearance.

Mo killed the ball under his studs and swept a clinical finish away from Pat Bonner.

McCoist was later to joke that he finally caught up with the ecstatic Johnston at Cessnock Underground as he tried to join in the celebrations!

It was to be the goal that made him at Rangers and Johnston confessed: "That was the moment that made me feel accepted as a Rangers player.

"It had been such an important decision to make to come to Rangers, I knocked Souness back three times before I decided that I could handle it.

'That goal made me feel I was a Ranger'

"But after my mind was made up, I was confident that after all the hype everything would fall into place once I actually started playing."

Johnston's belief had been backed up when over 5,000 fans were locked out when he made his Ibrox debut in a friendly against Spurs.

It had been bolstered when he was hailed by

many after that header against the Dons.

But it wasn't until that critical goal that it was confirmed – he had crossed one of the bitterest divides of football in the eyes of the bulk of the Rangers support.

And he recalled: "It was the perfect way to prove to critics that I would do the business for Rangers – no matter who we were playing.

"Some said I'd never score against Celtic but I did it with two minutes to go and it was the goal that put us top of the league.

"At all my clubs – from Partick Thistle to Kansas City Wizard – there have been important goals that have helped me. That was perhaps the most important of my Ibrox career."

Four tension-packed months had passed since the dramatic days when a controversial U-turn on a Celtic move paved the way for his sensational switch to Gers.

In those early days, Johnston assumed a higher profile than the Prime Minister – and he had the bodyguards to go with it. Burly minders shielded the flame-haired star everywhere he went amid allegations of death threats, but he remained more concerned about breaking his scoring duck for the club.

He insisted: "Rangers were comfortable for me to have protection but I didn't really think I needed it.

"They said I'd never show my face in Glasgow again after the transfer but within a week I was up seeing my mum!

DON FOR...
Mo Johnston
powers home
a header for
his first goal
for Rangers

'Souness was sure he had a team of champions'

"I was honestly more worried about life on the park and, after waiting for seven games, I felt a huge wave of relief when I scored against the Dons.

"I still laugh with Alex McLeish when he recalls one of his diehard mates saying they'd got a good point at Ibrox.

"Eck said: 'What do you mean? It was 1-0,' and the guy replied as quick as a flash that as far as he was concerned the goal didn't count!

"So I knew I had battles to win but I like to think that goal against Celtic set me on the way."

Now MoJo was flying and he was on target again alongside the gifted Mark Walters in a 2-0 win over Dundee that set them up for the first treacherous trip to Pittodrie. The Light Blues played some of their best football of the season but still perished with Hans Gillhaus' goal clinching it – yet Souness walked out convinced he had a team of champions on his hands once more.

November 25 brought what should have been a routine home clash with Dunfermline. However, it was transformed into an extraordinary occasion by the departure of a player who remains in the fans' hearts to this day.

Doubts had surrounded Souness' judgement when former England skipper Ray Wilkins arrived from French club Paris St Germain two years earlier — Razor dispelled every one.

The man who had seen it all at Chelsea, Manchester

United and AC Milan was 31 when he checked into the hurly-burly of Scottish football. But he still had the class and passing vision in abundance to leave the signature of a midfield artist when he quit to return south to Queen's Park Rangers.

The mist swirled around Ibrox as Wilkins bade farewell in the best way possible, helping Rangers to a 3-0 win, topped off by another sublime pass that set up Johnston to net once more.

And Ray revealed: "I have a portrait of myself playing for Rangers that the club presented me with that day and it remains one of my proudest possessions.

"It was a difficult occasion in many ways – you get this image as a hard-bitten pro, but I was in floods of tears as I left the pitch. It was very emotional.

"My wife Jackie and I have been lucky enough to

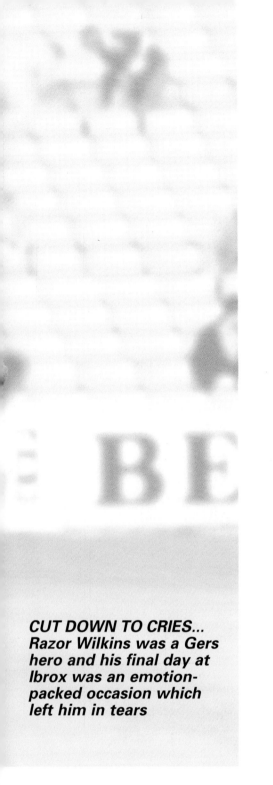

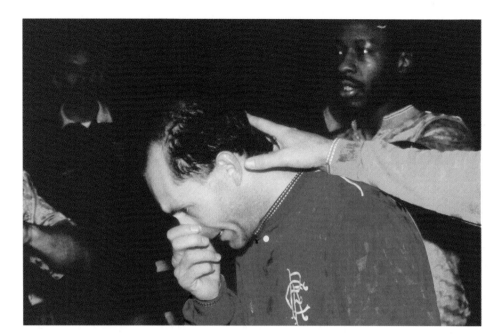

'I decided I wanted to go out at the top'

CUT DOWN TO CRIES...
Razor Wilkins was a Gers hero and his final day at Ibrox was an emotion-packed occasion which left him in tears

take the family to some marvellous places throughout my career but those two-and-a-half years at Ibrox were among the happiest."

The legacy of Wilkins' influence lives on at Ibrox, eight years after he walked out the exit door. Ian Ferguson and Ian Durrant are still quick to remember the lessons that moulded them into better players.

Not even turning up to play for Hibs against his old club last season could sour his Gers love affair. He went off to a standing ovation.

BUT ask him why he didn't stick around longer and the cold-eyed professionalism of a winner capped 84 times for England glints through.

He shrugged simply: "I didn't want to outstay my welcome. I looked around the dressing-room and saw the likes of Ian Ferguson and Durrant and the others coming through and knew I might end up playing a minimal part.

"I didn't want Rangers fans to remember Ray running up and down the sidelines in a sub's tracksuit, so I went out at the top."

Souness made a shrewd dip into the transfer market immediately to land former Liverpool star Nigel Spackman from QPR – and Wilkins believes that was the measure of the man.

The Rangers gaffer was to look back and insist he'd bought Wilkins as much for his influence in the dressing-room as his undoubted quality on the park.

And it worked – Ray had the respect of Ibrox inner sanctum and wide-eyed youngsters and experienced

Wilkins had gone but Rangers rolled on

stars alike listened to how the proper diet and fitness work helped you cope in Serie A.

The gospel that Souness himself preached from his days with Sampdoria was being hammered home again.

Ray admitted: "That was Graeme's big strength for me, getting people to do a specific job.

"He was clever to spot that perhaps I could have a say in the dressing-room where he couldn't because he had to distance himself as manager and the spirit that season was fantastic.

"They knew when to laugh, like the day I wrote "Shilts – England's No.1!" on the inside of Chris Woods' shinpads!

"But they were winners too, because Chris then went out and played brilliantly to prove to me he really did deserve the jersey ahead of Peter Shilton."

Wilkins left Rangers with cheers ringing in his ears and a locker full of memories, including the greatest goal of his illustrious career.

He grinned: "That came in the 5-1 win over Celtic in August 1988 when I hit one of the best volleys of my life.

"You know when you've caught a ball just right and that was on the sweet spot because I hardly felt it leave my boot. It roared in and then I was off and running. The celebrations that day even topped those when I scored for Manchester United in the FA Cup Final against Brighton.

"Yep, it was without question the fastest I've ever run in my life!"

Wilkins was gone but Rangers rolled on and Hearts were beaten 2-1 at Ibrox before the centre stage that Ray had graced on his big day was filled by one of its most prolific performers.

Ally McCoist doesn't just merit an entry in the Rangers record books – he tends to rewrite them.

And December 9 was no different as the Johnston-McCoist partnership clicked once more in a 3-0 win over Motherwell.

Butcher's searching long ball found Johnston coming off his marker to take a boot in the back of the calf but still cushion a perfect lay-off into his partner's path.

The chip from 20 yards was vintage McCoist and the ball floated over the despairing Ally Maxwell.

It was the 128th Premier League goal of Ally's career and beat the previous mark set by Frank McGarvey.

Next time up it was Johnston who salvaged a vital point at Tannadice before a goal in a rare sub's appearance from Davie Dodds clinched a 1-0 home win over St Mirren.

Hibs then put up the shutters in a frustrating 0-0 draw at Easter Road before the New Year clash at Parkhead – and a dream Old Firm debut for Spackman.

Celts desperately needed the points to stay in the running, but McCoist broke clear to smack the ball across goal and there was Spackman to rap home from close range.

It was to be his only goal in 21 league games that season – but what a time to score it!

As Spacks rang in a Happy Blue Year, Rangers were grinding into gear for what was to become their trademark – the festive form that leaves their rivals floundering.

Souness' side lost just once in five months as the title was clinched and January brought four

44

WOOD YOU BELIEVE IT... Ray Wilkins shared a dressing room jibe with his fellow countryman

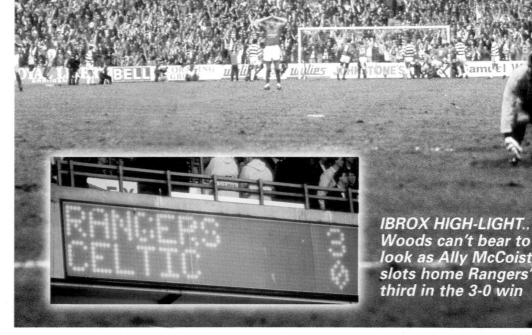

straight wins.

Walters left Aberdeen beaten and bewildered with a classic strike in a 2-0 win a Ibrox before Dundee were humbled 3-0 and a collector's piece Gary Stevens goal sealed victory at Dunfermline.

January also brought a milestone for skipper Butcher with the birth of his third son on January 16.

And he revealed: "We called him Alistair Ian after McCoist and Durrant so it was always guaranteed that he'd grow up a BAMPOT!"

Terry, of course, had been in the first party of Englishmen who'd come north when the Souness Revolution began in 1986.

And he fell in love with Scotland so much that when the sack as manager at Coventry and Sunderland left him bereft he returned north to lick his wounds and start a new career as Mine Host at the Old Manor Hotel in Bridge of Allan.

THE title drive under Tel soared on with Chris Vinnicombe deputising for the skipper in a 3-1 win over Dundee United.

McCoist netted again with blood streaming from a head wound and struck a celebration pose that was to launch a thousand bootleg T-shirts up for grabs along Edmiston Drive on matchday.

All of a sudden, though, the well-oiled machine began to cough and splutter on February 10.

The diminutive figure of Motherwell's Dougie Arnott has plagued a string of Rangers' stoppers throughout the years — certainly Butcher and Richard Gough would never list the striker who came up the hard way at Pollok Juniors as their favourite rival.

He struck that day and Rangers were reeling on the ropes until Johnston once more came to the rescue to bludgeon home a volley in a 1-1 draw.

The rot had started, though, and points were jettisoned in successive draws with Hearts, Dundee and St Mirren before the stunning shock of home defeat from Hibs.

Seven months on from the day he smashed a goal beyond Bonni Ginzburg, Keith Houchen was terrorising Rangers again and the heat was cranked up as the final Old Firm league clash of the season beckoned.

Rangers had been in cruise control, now the chips were down. Souness took his side away to Gleneagles for a break from the pressure but Johnston recalled: "I sat in the dressing-room that day before the match and knew there would only be one winner.

"We'd been well out in front and now there was a danger of it all blowing up in our faces.

"So the determination was incredible and in the end we won 3-0 going on 5-0."

Celtic defender Anton Rogan seemed to view these clashes as his personal chance to commit soccer suicide and this was no different.

Butcher hoisted a hopeful cross towards the back post and for no apparent reason the Irishman blatantly punched clear – penalty!

Walters rode his luck as Bonner's firm hand deflected his effort high into the net but Rangers were off and running.

Then came a goal that showcased the predatory instincts of a partnership that was soon to be brutally broken up.

McCoist, whose ability outside the box has so often been under-rated, gathered and sped wide before angling a precise chip onto Johnston's chest.

One touch to control and a dipping volley was ripping into the far corner for a goal that captured the footballing telepathy Mo and Ally had that season.

The icing on the cake was McCoist's second-half penalty which gave him the post-war record of league goals for the club, a mark he had held jointly with Derek Johnstone.

Yet it was a double act living on borrowed time and Mo still firmly believes boss Souness got it WRONG when he split up the deadly duo for the following campaign.

He sighed: "That was what had swung my move for me in the first place, the prospect of playing alongside Ally was the deciding factor.

"And for me it worked, we had an exceptional part-

'Butcher fell in love with Scotland'

nership because we toiled long and hard on the training ground perfecting the runs we'd make for each other.

"The next season Graeme told me it was to be myself and Mark Hateley and although it worked I have to say I felt that the change WASN'T needed.

"It's a regret that Ally and I were only given one full season together and I really felt for him as the next season went on and he spent most of the time on the bench.

"The team changed its outlook then and I felt we lost a bit."

A 0-0 draw at Aberdeen was followed by a scare when Nick Cusack headed Motherwell in front at Ibrox.

But Rangers dredged into their reserves again and Trevor Steven's acrobatic volley dragged them level within 60 seconds before Johnston grabbed yet another priceless winner.

And so to Tannadice on April 21, 1990 and the crowning glory of a season that had fizzed and crackled since Johnston's signing turned Scottish football on its head.

Yet Butcher believes Rangers' championship glory owed a lot to one of the club's real unsung heroes.

Stuart Munro was a modest investment for Rangers, plucked from Alloa in the bad, old days of 1984 when Brasso for the Trophy Room wasn't high on the Ibrox shopping list.

But he learned to prosper amid the Souness all-stars and the popular left-back was an ever-present that season, his 36 league games marked by a cupboard full of Player of the Year awards from grateful fans.

It was fitting then that he should play a key role in the goal that won the

BLOOD, SWEAT AND CHEERS... *Butcher summed up the winning spirit at the new Ibrox*

UNSUNG HERO....
Stuart Munro played a key part in Rangers' title push

'Souness changed the face of Scottish football'

title and Butcher recalled: "That was a true item for the collector.

"Not only did we see a right foot cross from Stuart Munro but we also saw a header from Trevor Steven – unbelievable.

"Seriously, Stuart was such a valuable player. There were no frills with him but he did a great job."

This was to be the last title Butcher savoured as Rangers captain and he can still remember every minute detail seven years on.

He said: "The full-time whistle blew with the ball at my feet and I just remember picking it up and thinking it was over, we'd done it.

"It was such a thrill and we had the mother of all parties in the smallest away dressing-room I've ever seen!

"We stopped at the Swallow Hotel on the way out of Dundee and in true Souness style Graeme bought the boys a round - champagne, of course.

"Yet, to be honest, I felt it was a disappointing season in some ways.

"The season before we'd been heading for the Treble only to lose the Scottish Cup Final to Celtic.

"Even then the level of expectation at Ibrox was enormous and I really felt Rangers shouldn't be satisfied with just one trophy."

A 2-0 victory over Dunfe-

rmline and a 1-1 draw with Hearts, featuring Munro's first goal of the season, brought the season to a close.

BUTCHER jetted out to Italia '90 where he helped England to the verge of the World Cup Final– when he returned his champagne days at Rangers were to lose their fizz.

Ironically, it was at Tannadice – the scene of one of his most memorable triumphs five months earlier – that was to become the graveyard of Terry Butcher's

Rangers career in September 1990.

He backheaded a bizarre own goal beyond Chris Woods in a 2-1 defeat and was dropped for the Skol Cup semi-final with Aberdeen four days later - he never played for Rangers again.

The axeing of a man who had become a Light Blues legend made front page news and Butcher was eventually sent to Coventry in a £400,000 move.

There's deep sadness now at the way it all ended and Terry groaned: "There are certainly things I would have done differently and I think things Graeme would have done differently.

"It ended up a very bad move for me because I got the sack as Coventry manager in the end and those heady days at Rangers seemed a long way away."

Yet despite the bitter ending to his Rangers adventure Terry still has the utmost respect for the man who took football's biggest sleeping giant by the throat and shook it back to life.

"Souness is the main reason I

became a Rangers player," said Butcher.

"I admired him both as a player and a manager and there is NO-ONE who could have persuaded me to come to Scotland in 1986 other than Graeme Souness.

"At Rangers he changed the whole face of Scottish football.

"And I believe if that's the way he's always remembered then that should be enough."

49

McEWAN'S
IT'S WHAT WE STAND FOR.

Explore new dimensions in time.

"1911" in steel and 18K gold. Water resistant to 30m.
5 year international warranty.

EBEL
The Architects of Time

ision Champions 1990-91

This chapter is brought to you
in association with

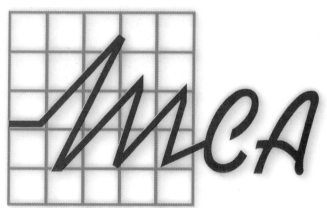

(Multi-Media) Ltd.
inc. MCA CC TV Systems

THREE IN A ROW Mark H ele

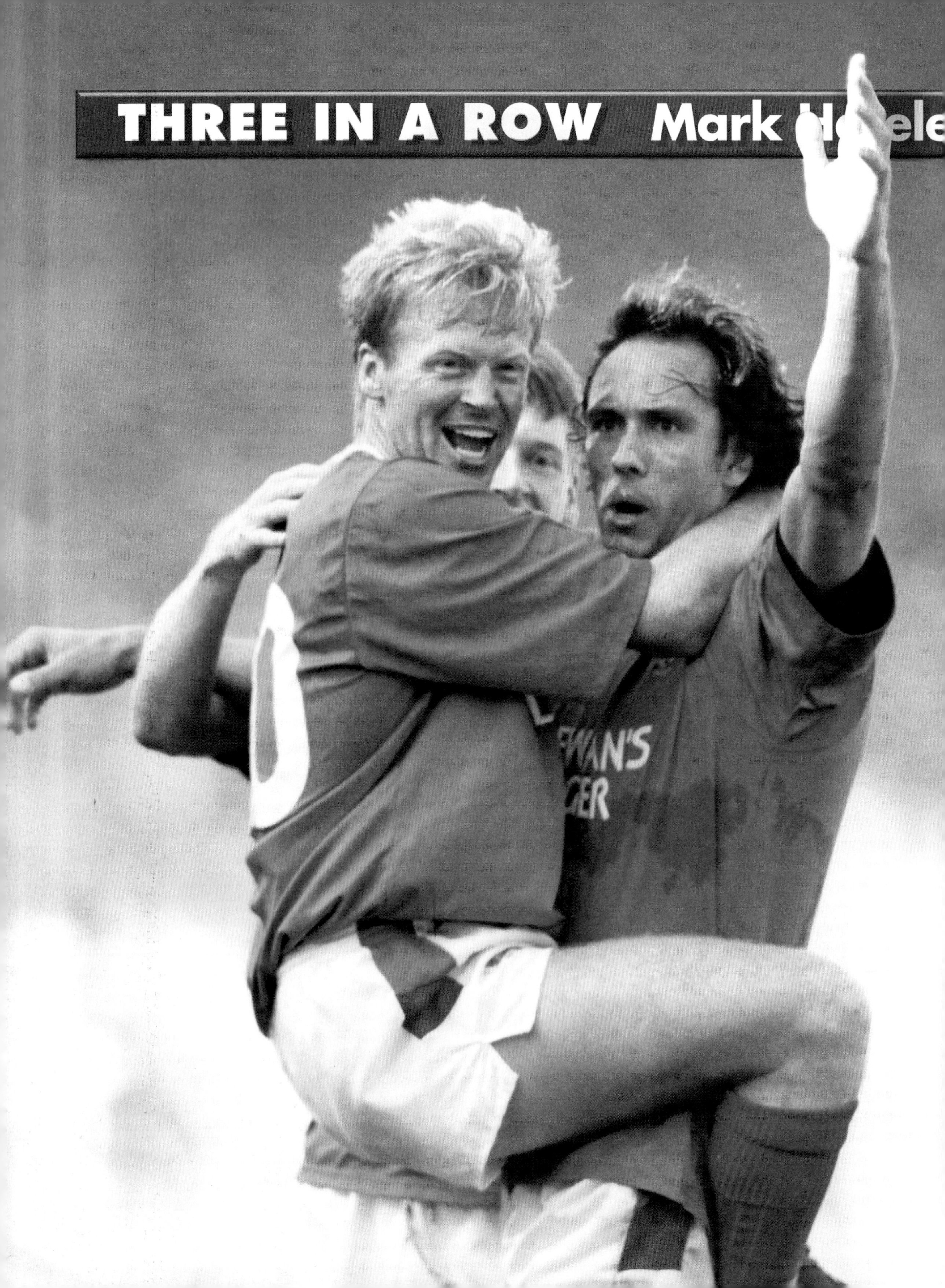

CHAPTER 3

NEVER again will the emotions of those who love Rangers be stripped as raw as they were throughout these ten traumatic months. The early pain caused by skipper Terry Butcher's departure was eased by new captain Richard Gough's crucial contribution in dumping Celtic to secure the Skol Cup.

But the club was to be bombed out of Europe by Red Star Belgrade and by April 16, 1991, the players were stunned and reeling. Hot on the heels of humbling back-to-back defeats by the Hoops in the Scottish Cup and the League came the news that shocked Scottish football to the core – Graeme Souness had quit for Liverpool.

He left a club in turmoil, but lifelong Rangers fan Walter Smith was promoted from his role as Souness' right-hand man to guide his side to the title in the biggest league game Scottish football has ever seen.

So long Souness, welcome Walter

RANGERS v Aberdeen, May 11, 1991 – the two clubs who could take the title head-to-head in a winner-takes-all final day showdown. It was to be a match that will never be forgotten.

Mark Hateley will forever be cast as the hero whose goals gave Rangers the Championship on one of the most dramatic days in Scottish football history.

But it shouldn't be forgotten that before he won the title, the combative Englishman first had to win over a disenchanted band of fans left bereft when their idol Ally McCoist was cast aside.

Super Ally was now supersub as Graeme Souness plumped for Hateley and Maurice Johnston up

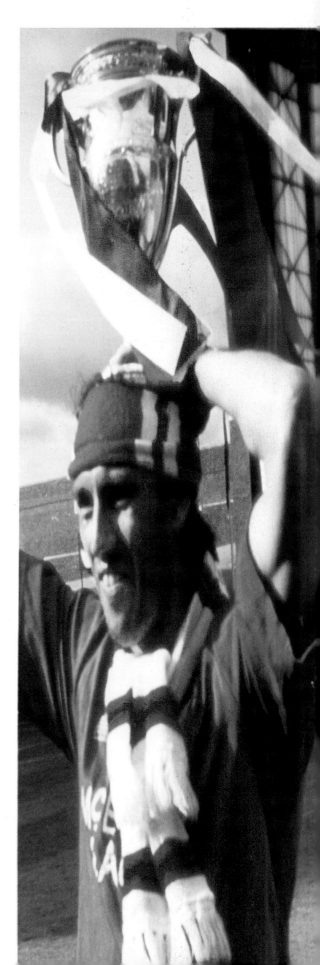

IN DUTCH... Ally McCoist (No.9) celebrates a goal with new signing Pieter Huistra

'Ally was on the bench so often he was known as The Judge'

front. For many fans, big Mark was the villain guilty of booting McCoist on to the bench. Ally sat there so many times that season he was eventually nicknamed "The Judge".

Hateley had been part of another Souness summer cash splash and the £1 million the manager paid Monaco looked a sound investment when he careered onto John Brown's cross and rammed a text-book header beyond Andy Rhodes in a 3-1 opening win at home to Dunfermline.

Two players of vastly-contrasting style joined Hateley on a Scottish adventure.

Pieter Huistra, full of wing daring and the deftest touches, arrived from Dutch side FC Twente Enshede and hard man Terry Hurlock – who was full of no such traits – bulldozed in from Millwall.

The signature of classy Russian Oleg Kuznetsov had also been guaranteed for £1.2m, although he would not arrive from Dynamo Kiev until October.

McCoist watched from the sidelines as Hateley lapped up that dream Ibrox start against the Pars, but Mark knew trouble was just around the corner.

He explained: "The big problem I had when I arrived was that I'd been out injured for the best part of 18 months at Monaco.

"My ankle had been totally reconstructed and I knew I'd take time to get back into the swing of things.

"I also knew Ally was a hero and it was hard for the fans to accept that he was on the bench.

"But the thing was when I got fit I knew I would play, because Graeme wanted to have a target man.

"It really wasn't me who was replacing McCoist, it was Mo Johnston because, in the Souness way of thinking, I was the one who was a cert to play."

Hateley's sense of foreboding was justified. He wasn't fully match-fit and a blank in the 0-0 draw at Hibs was to become a familiar story in those difficult

RUSSIAN ROULETTE...
Oleg Kuznetsov's £1.2million move to Rangers took a tragic twist after just two games

TERRY'S ALL BOLD...
Hurlock shows some
of the grit which
made him popular
with Ibrox fans – but
feared by his rivals

'At last, Souness had found someone as hard as him'

early days. After that Ibrox strike on his home debut, he didn't score another league goal for over two months and the fury over McCoist's fate threatened to split the support apart at times.

Ally was back in favour with a bang on September 8 at Tynecastle and the penalty box predator showed he still had what it takes.

The 3-1 win over Hearts was embroidered with two classic McCoist finishes – a nutmeg on Henry Smith after a superb Johnston pass and a snapping volley from Hateley's knockdown.

For now, his uneasy relationship with Souness was at peace – it wasn't to last.

The first Old Firm game of the season at Ibrox brought a 1-1 draw and goals from two players who'd have been last on your coupon for first to score.

Derek Whyte nodded Celtic in front, but Rangers picked up a point thanks to a deflected 20-yard drive from Hurlock.

The 32-year-old Cockney journeyman with the bubble perm seemed a bizarre Souness signing.

Yet he was to get 29 league games, a vital contribution and the full value of his £300,000 investment in the former England B star back before offloading him to Southampton the following season.

And, at last, the manager had also found someone who was as hard as him!

Single-minded Souness refused to flinch from testing decisions in the Ibrox hotseat – and one of the toughest was looming.

As the manager watched

'Woods showed why he was put in goals as a kid'

his team crumble to a 2-1 defeat at Tannadice on September 22, he'd decided skipper Terry Butcher's Rangers career was over.

After all the glory that had gone before, it was heartbreaking that his last act should be to stretch awkwardly for Billy Thomson's kick-out and send a header over Chris Woods for a comedy-cuts own-goal.

With a midweek Skol Cup semi-final against Aberdeen to face, Souness acted swiftly and Butcher was axed.

THE man who had been the heartbeat of the club was nowhere to be seen at Hampden Park. Richard Gough accept-

ed the captain's mantle and matchwinner Trevor Steven inspired Rangers to victory. Souness stoically faced the criticism over the manner of Butcher's bulleting and, six weeks later, Terry was sent to Coventry in a £400,000 move.

Behind the scenes, Hateley had seen further confirmation of the manager's iron will to win at all costs.

Mark stressed: "I don't

NO SWEAT … Trevor Steven fired Rangers into the Skol Cup final

KEEP AWAY... Chris Woods could afford to miss a penalty against Valetta in the European Cup – Rangers won 10-0 on aggregate anyway!

think anyone else but Graeme Souness could have turned round Rangers as quickly as he did. He had this attitude that he was going to be a winner, no matter what.

"If he upset people, then so be it – he had a goal and he stuck to it.

"Believe me, it needed a figure like him to come in as manager and persuade the Terry Butchers and the like to come to Scotland in the first place. Souness had proved himself as a player at every level and had that allure that made you want to work with him."

With Steven's influence growing at the heart of the midfield, John Brown steadied the ship in the league to edge a 1-0 Ibrox win over Motherwell, but Rangers ended September a point behind pacesetters Dundee United.

The European Cup adventure started with a 4-0 success against Valetta in Malta and the return at Ibrox in the teeming rain brought a goal for rookie John Spencer on his competitive debut.

Rangers' 6-0 win featured a hat-trick for Johnston and it would have been even more comprehensive if Woods hadn't shown why he was stuck in goals as a kid by squirting a penalty yards wide. A goal-less league draw at Aberdeen was the precursor to a long-awaited Ibrox debut for Kuznetsov against St Mirren on October 13 — and Oleg didn't disappoint.

Anyone who witnessed that 90 minutes must still feel cheated all these years on – they were given a fleeting glimpse of what might have been.

Kuznetsov strutted imperiously, snuffing out danger

MIXED FORTUNES... Kuznetsov's career never recovered from this injury while (right) Hateley just got better and better

'Oleg was never the same player again'

in defence and striding forward to spray passes before shelling a 30-yarder off the post.

The champions won 5-0, with doubles from McCoist and Mark Walters and another goal from Johnston.

And the verdict was unanimous – the Russian looked like a legend in the making.

Yet, 20 minutes into the next match at St Johnstone, he caught his studs in the McDiarmid Park turf and his season was finished.

The 0-0 draw that day paled into insignificance when the extent of the damage to Kuznetsov's knee became apparent. He was never the same player again.

A 3-0 mauling in Yugoslavia from eventual European Cup winners Red Star Belgrade plunged Rangers further into the depths of depression.

But this was to be a season marked by a dogged refusal to bow to mounting pressures and Rangers stormed back to claim the Skol Cup in dramatic fashion against Celtic four days later.

Gough's first final as the Light Blues' captain became a fairytale. If I had been working for *Roy of the Rovers*, they'd have thrown the script back in my face.

The lion-hearted Paul Elliott rocked Rangers when he stooped to divert a header beyond Woods but McCoist teed up Walters to take the tie into extra-time.

A long, hopeful ball from Gary Stevens found Hateley engaged in aerial warfare with Elliott, although neither got a touch as the ball skidded through.

Packie Bonner and Chris Morris hesitated and Gough stole in to prod the ball over the line before he joyfully

hurdled the hoardings to party at the Rangers end.

Butcher would never leave the fans' hearts, but a new skipper had started his era in style.

Europe, though, was once more a lost cause and the punters knew it.

Only 23,831 turned up to marvel at the skills of Red Star's Robert Prosinecki and Darko Pancev, who scored a memorable volley, as McCoist's header salvaged some pride in a 1-1 second leg draw.

The boost from winning the first silverware of the season fuelled a 4-0 win over Hibs on November 3 that at last brought Hateley a welcome double.

He had waited since that first game against Dunfermline to hit the target in the league.

Mark had an army of doubters back then – but he was not among their ranks.

He insisted: "The biggest problem I had was joining when I wasn't fully fit, but I always knew it would come good for me at Rangers.

"That's one of the main pieces of baggage I've carried throughout my career – a mental toughness and self-belief.

"For me, that is what you need most to be a success at Ibrox.

"Sure, there were tough times in that first season, but I was always confident I could win the fans round."

The wheels came off at home to Dundee United the following Saturday, when

Darren Jackson's double sent Rangers spinning to defeat, despite a lashing left-foot volley from McCoist.

Ally was back on the bench at Fir Park, where right-back Gary Stevens grabbed a double in a thrilling 4-2 win.

That was to be the start of a hugely significant run as Rangers went 15 games and almost four months without a league defeat.

Hateley secured the points at Dunfermline before the trip to Parkhead on November 25 that confirmed Johnston's thirst for goals knew no bounds.

As Lex Baillie's misplaced header spiralled down, Mo must have felt the animosity spilling towards him as Bonner advanced.

But he was the coolest man in the stadium under the leaden Glasgow skies.

The lob was perfect and Rangers were one up until that man Elliott smashed home a header from a wicked John Collins free-kick.

Now Souness' side needed a winner. They got it from the man Rangers kept in part-time employment.

Hurlock mugged Stevie Fulton in midfield and, as the Celtic bench erupted in fury, sub McCoist was already off and running to collect the pass.

Ally's nerve held true and he dummied Bonner onto his backside before planting the ball home and celebrating with a dance like a robot in a trance behind the goal. The weird moves belonged to a Gary Numan video, but after all he'd been through, McCoist could be forgiven the extravagance.

Ally was on the bench – and came on to score again – in a 4-0 home win over Hearts that was quickly followed by a 4-1 Ibrox drubbing of St Johnstone.

Hateley, Johnston and Walters – by now firmly established as Souness' Three Amigos up front – were all on target in a 3-0 win over St Mirren before December 22 brought the clearest indication that McCoist's rift with the manager would never be healed.

ALLY came off the bench again at home to Aberdeen to accept a Stevens throw on his chest, evade Brian Irvine and send an unbelievable left-foot hitch-kick past Theo Snelders.

It might just be the best goal he's ever scored for Rangers but as chairman David Murray was later to confirm, a stern-faced Souness couldn't bring himself to applaud.

McCoist netted again but Jim Bett struck twice to smuggle a 2-2 draw and the writing was on the wall for the Rangers' fans' favourite. The next week at Tannadice saw him consigned to the subs' bench once more.

Johnston and Walters sent Rangers out of 1990 clear in the title race and on a high after a 2-1 win.

But for Ally, these were the darkest days at Ibrox since Jock Wallace offered him a move to Cardiff as he struggled badly to win over the fans seven years earlier.

Hateley, though, believes it was during those soul-searching days that McCoist

steeled himself to stay positive and build the foundations for what was to become the greatest Rangers striking partnership of modern times.

Mark pointed out: "Ally is a clever guy and I feel in some strange ways that season spent mostly on the sidelines was good for him.

"He's since told me that he used it to watch and learn and one of the things he took on board from me was how to up his work-rate outside the box.

"Before then, he'd only come alive when he was given a chance to show his finishing power. I like to think I made him a better all-round striker.

"Ally would always ask me about my experiences in Europe and look for things to help him improve."

New Year has traditionally brought Rangers the chance to give their cross-city rivals a kick up the bells in recent years and 1991 was no different, although the first goal came from a huge slice – literally – of luck.

Walters' studs caught in the turf and that gave his right-foot corner the vicious dip and swerve that took it in at the near post past the despairing Bonner.

A horrendous blunder from Peter Grant then sent 19-year-old midfielder Sandy Robertson clear and he skipped round the helpless Packie to give Hateley a late Christmas present four yards out.

Now Rangers were on the boil and the patience and passing that Souness had drilled into the club since his arrival five years earlier were stamped all over a classic goal. Ironically, it's one that few will remember.

It came at Tynecastle on January 5 and, although the seconds were ticking away amid the howling wind and

'I like to think that I made McCoist a better striker'

rain, the champs still kept the ball on the deck through 11 passes that filleted Hearts.

Finally, Johnston set up Walters for one of those trademark double shuffles and the cross was meat and drink to Hateley, who swept home a right-foot shot from close range.

Meanwhile, away from the glare of the fans – or at least that's the way it was planned – a very special player was preparing for his comeback.

Two-and-a-half years after the awful moment when Aberdeen's Neil Simpson lost the plot and smashed his studs into Ian Durrant's knee, the gifted midfielder was back in a light blue jersey.

It was only a reserve match against Hibs, but it brought astonishing scenes as over 15,000 fans turned up to welcome him back.

They caught the club by surprise and some had to be led round the track to their seats because not enough gates had been opened. It was a gesture from the hearts of a support who

knew the player needed their help on the hard road back from his personal hell.

Back on the top team front, Dunfermline were beaten 2-0 at Ibrox before a similar result at Hibs, where Chris Vinnicombe notched his first and only league goal for the club.

McCOIST was back for his first start in 12 games at home to St Mirren on February 9 and responded in typical style, cottoning on to Spencer's flick to score with an acrobatic volley.

The next game with Motherwell gave Hateley and McCoist – the men who would torment defences all over Europe in years to come – a rare chance to link up.

Poor Ally Maxwell, who would later become a Rangers team-mate, was the man to suffer as the double act both plundered goals with exquisite lobs as the champs disposed of Mother-

well. For big Mark, it was a sign of things to come and he smiled: "Our partnership after Mo left was frightening. I learned more about the art of scoring from Ally and I helped him to Golden Boots and everything – we were so good for each other.

"If you keyed details into a computer and looked for two strikers with the perfect attributes to play together, it would come up with Hateley and McCoist."

Huistra – who was to spend much of his first season on the bench adapting to Scottish football – chipped in with a goal to earn a 1-1 draw at St Johnstone before Rangers' unbeaten record perished at Pittodrie.

Hans Gillhaus' strike snatched it for the Dons and, although Rangers battled back with a 2-1 win over Hearts, disaster was about to strike on successive Sundays at Parkhead.

First, on March 17, the Scottish Cup run ended in shame with Walters, Hateley and Hurlock being sent off with Celtic's Peter Grant as goals from Gerry Creaney

'Smith knew something was nagging his preoccupied gaffer'

and Dariusz Wdowczyk gave the Hoops a 2-0 triumph.

As if that wasn't bad enough, McCoist was posted missing altogether this time, disciplined by the manager for making a trip to Cheltenham races.

He was told to make a public apology and relations with Souness were now at an all-time low.

Ally was later to smile: "I came out of my local chippy at that time very downcast and I was wandering sadly up the road.

"Then came the cry 'Haw McCoist – you were the only Rangers player at the races the other day!'.

"Humour like that will always keep you going."

McCoist was back in for the league clash, which was not the same high-pressure affair.

But the suspensions from the woeful first match hit hard and Rangers were trounced 3-0 as Joe Miller, Anton Rogan and Tommy Coyne found the target.

The news that the influential Trevor Steven was out for the rest of the season with injury simply sealed a miserable spell for the crestfallen Souness.

No-one could have known then, but time was beginning to run out on his Rangers' reign.

Now the heat was on and only a brilliant volleyed finish from Gary Stevens, after

ALL CHANGE...
Rogan scores in Celtic's 3-0 Old Firm win on St Patrick's Day, Souness departs for Anfield and Smith leads Rangers to the league title

Hateley's shot had been parried, plundered the points from Dunfermline.

That good work was ruined as they marked Ian Durrant's return to the first team by flopping in a 0-0 draw with Hibs at Ibrox.

Inside the club, trouble was brewing in the wake of Kenny Dalglish's decision to quit Liverpool as the strain of the disasters of Heysel and Hillsborough took their toll.

Souness was the man the Anfield chiefs wanted and before Rangers' next home game with St Johnstone on April 13, there was a whirlwind of activity in the corridors of power.

Walter Smith knew something was nagging at his preoccupied gaffer and it wasn't long before he found out what.

HE recalled: "When you work together as manager and assistant, it's a very close relationship – you discuss most things.

"I remember Kenny leaving Liverpool and a few days later Graeme broke the news – he'd been asked to take the job.

"Three weeks later, after all the reaction to Kenny's departure had died down,

they got in touch again. He said he was going to meet them and came back up and said he was leaving.

"Graeme said 'If you want, you can come with me'. I wasn't sure about that, but I didn't know if I'd be offered the job at Ibrox, so I couldn't dismiss it out of hand."

When the chance to join Rangers came his way in 1986, Smith had wrenched himself away after 20 years at Dundee United.

Souness' association with Rangers had lasted just five years, but he was no less committed and Smith sympathised as the manager went through agony trying to make the right decision.

Walter revealed: "Graeme told the physio Phil Boersma and I in the morning that he was going to tell the chairman in the afternoon he was going.

"They had a close relationship and I think Graeme felt he could stay until the end of the season and go. The chairman decided to act more promptly than that.

"It was indicated that he should go there and then and it left me wondering what I was going to do.

"But it really never crossed my mind to go to Liverpool. I'd already had five years as no.2 at Tannadice and five years in the same role at Ibrox.

"If there was any chance

of getting the job at Rangers then I was going nowhere."

Smith soon knew how his future would look. Faced with a crisis – as he has been a thousand times in business – Murray acted swiftly and surely.

The Rangers manager said: "On the night the story broke, the chairman phoned me and told me to see him the next day.

"It was a Friday and he said: 'This has just happened, so give me time – but don't worry too much'.

"We had a home game with St Johnstone on the Saturday and that morning David Murray came into Ibrox and offered me the job as Rangers manager.

"Just 36 hours after Graeme left, I'd been given the chance to manage the club I loved."

NOT surprisingly, Murray wanted to delay the announcement until after the clash with Saints.

Smith could afford to concentrate on team matters and ignore Press speculation linking everyone from Franz Beckenbauer to Johan Cruyff to the vacancy.

On the field, the players were single-minded and, despite a harsh red card for young defender Brian Reid – Souness' last signing from Morton – they cruised to a 3-0 win.

The high point came as Durrant tricked away from his marker and curled home a left-foot shot. The joy on his face as he ran to celebrate remains one of the images of that season.

Spencer also notched his first league goal and Huistra wrapped it up.

Soon, however, the players' minds would return to other business.

Five years after he had turned our game upside down and breathed life back into Rangers, Souness was gone. The players were stunned.

Hateley recalled: "I thought it was a wind-up when we were told he'd quit. It was just so out of the blue.

"I was flabbergasted but I had a chat with David Murray and I had no hesitation in telling him Walter was his man.

"I have so much respect for him, both as a football manager and as a person."

It was Souness who had given Hateley the chance to rejuvenate his career in Glasgow – and stuck by him when he didn't make an instant impact.

When the parting came, Mark admits his initial shock was soon tempered by realism – Souness was simply a prisoner to his competitive nature.

THE big striker said: "It was sad to see Graeme close to tears when he left, but no-one should look back and blame him for going.

"He'd played at Liverpool and been a hero, and here he was being given the chance to manage them.

"They're a massive club and I think he felt he was constantly clashing with the SFA.

"I suspected he believed he'd taken Rangers as far as he could."

Now Smith faced the unenviable task of trying to impose his will on the team and calm the title jitters as the shock of Souness' departure sank in and the injuries mounted.

April 20 took Rangers to Love Street and a nerve-ridden game settled when

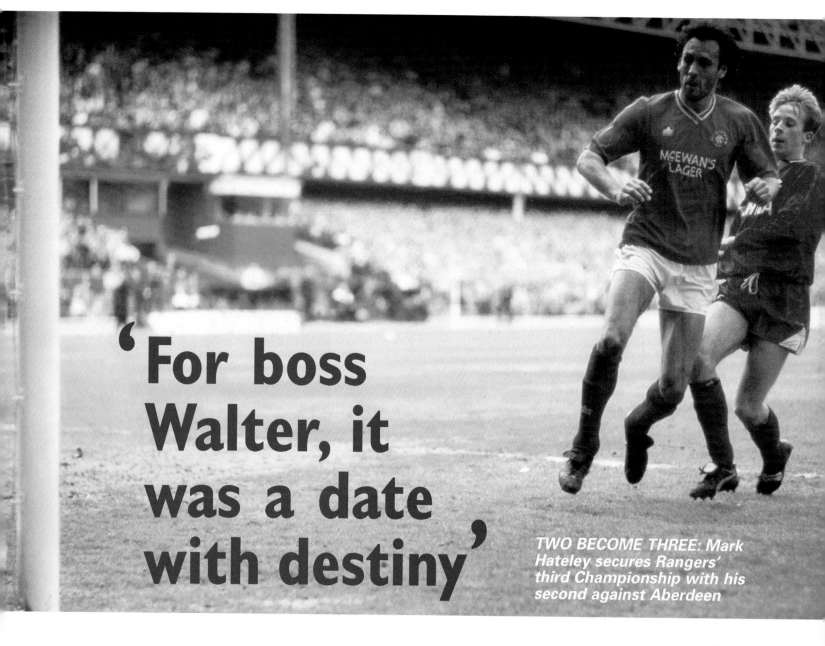

'For boss Walter, it was a date with destiny'

TWO BECOME THREE: *Mark Hateley secures Rangers' third Championship with his second against Aberdeen*

Stevens swung in a cross for kid midfielder Robertson.

One touch took Sandy out of harm's way and his volley nestled in the corner.

Smith had overcome the first hazardous hurdle and he confessed: "I knew then that if we didn't win the title, people could be on a downer on me from the start.

"But listen, jobs like being manager of Rangers don't come wrapped in Christmas paper.

"Sure, there were problems, but I preferred to look at it and say 'Okay, Graeme has left, but we can still win this Championship'."

Midweek brought Dundee United to Ibrox. By now, you could almost reach out and touch the tension in the air.

Ian Ferguson – who'd had another season bedevilled by injuries – settled it with a tremendously brave diving header that clinched another slender win.

The second last Saturday of the season began with Rangers travelling to Motherwell two points ahead of an Aberdeen side who'd dropped just one point from their last 22.

Alex Smith and Jocky Scott's side were to win 2-1 at home to St Johnstone – at Fir Park the roof fell in.

Archie Knox took his place in the dug-out as Smith's assistant for the first time, but it all went wrong when John Philliben blasted Motherwell ahead.

Huistra won a debatable penalty, only to see Walters blast it into the crowd. Dougie Arnott, so often a hammer of Rangers, rapped the nails into the coffin with two killer breakaway goals.

Now even Rangers' goal difference cushion had gone and the truth of their situation couldn't be simpler.

They were facing Aberdeen at Ibrox on the last day of the season and they had to win or the title dream was over after a season of triumph and trauma.

It was the first time since 1965, when Kilmarnock won at Hearts on the final day to take the title, that there had been a shootout on the last Saturday between the two championship contenders.

For boss Walter, it was a date with destiny, yet he

It was the day Hateley fell in love with the club for good

PAIN GAME…
John Brown (left)
snapped a tendon
during the
Aberdeen match,
but still
battled on to
enjoy the after
match sing-song

we were going into one of the biggest matches of our lives with the walking wounded.

"Even during the game Tom Cowan broke his leg and John Brown snapped his tendon and we had two more stretcher cases."

At the age of 20, Dons' stand-in keeper Michael Watt faced the most nerve-jangling afternoon of his life.

And battle-hardened pro Mark has no qualms about admitting he took advantage of that.

Hateley revealed: "I told Gary Stevens to throw in a high ball early on because I wanted to see what the kid was made of – legally of course!

"Gary did the business, I rattled into him and I don't think he ever really recovered.

"They got a free-kick but he got the message. I'd stamped my authority on him and, for kids growing up in a hard game, that's a lesson."

DUTCHMAN Peter van de Ven missed a sitter, feebly shooting straight at Woods as Rangers tried to defend without the floored Cowan, who had incredibly been playing on with that broken leg!

Van de Ven's country-man, Gillhaus, headed over before Hateley produced one of the moments that will go down in Rangers' folklore.

There seemed little danger when Walters took control on the left and slung over a long, hopeful cross five minutes from the break.

But big Mark stole a yard on marker Alex McLeish and leapt above him to power an astonishing header high past the flailing arms of Watt.

He roared away as the noise threatened to lift the roofs off the stands and he smiled: "It was my dream to score in that game before-hand but to score a goal of

that quality was a fantasy."

He added: "I sometimes stand before the picture of me running away to celebrate which hangs in my study and let my mind drift back to that day."

Yet still the injuries cursed Rangers after the break as Brown collapsed as if he'd been shot by a sniper in the stand.

His tendon had snapped and that meant the call for McCoist, half-fit and out of action for the past six weeks.

Hateley grinned: "That has to be my abiding memory of that day – Ally McWeeble, the 15-stone striker, wobbling on. I couldn't stop laughing!"

The patched-up champi-

ons, though, were calling the shots and, when Scott Booth's misplaced lay-off sent Johnston scurrying through after the break, Aberdeen were looking at the exit door.

Mo mis-hit the shot but, out of the corner of his eye, Watt could see Hateley thundering in.

And Mark insisted: "The second one came because Michael was looking for me before Mo even hit the shot.

"I believe that early challenge is why he fumbled a weak effort straight into my path to let me tie it all up."

After a season that stretched the nerves as taut as piano wires, the tunes of glory were once more bel-

lowing around Ibrox.

It was over and for the cosmopolitan strike star who had suffered through his battle for acceptance, it was the day he fell in love with a club for good.

HE stressed: "Rangers are the biggest and best club I have ever played for and that includes AC Milan.

"The greatest thing about it was that I became a real winner in Glasgow.

"I was able to use all the things I'd learned at Milan and Monaco and my education helped turn my experience into what I wanted – medals!

"And when I returned to Rangers it wasn't like coming back – it was like coming HOME."

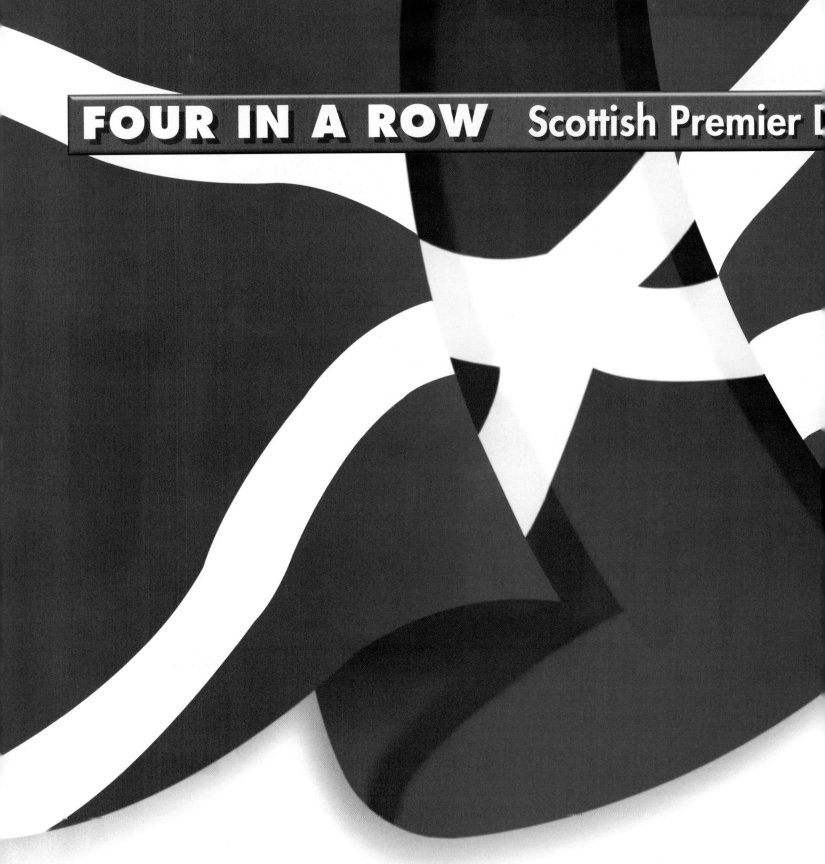

This chapter is brought to you
in association with

SCAFFOLDING

CHAPTER 4

IBROX had seen Struth, Symon and Souness – now it witnessed the dawn of the Smith Era. Five fraught matches on the title run-in after Souness' departure had been a high-pressure test of Walter's nerve in the hottest seat in Scottish football.

Now the real hard work began. As UEFA forced top clubs into playing just three foreigners in European ties, Smith was on his proving ground.

The new-look side lurched into an early week of crisis – blowing the Skol Cup semi-final against Hibs, losing to Aberdeen in the league and tumbling out of Europe against Sparta Prague.

But by the end of the season, the prolific pairing of Ally McCoist and Mark Hateley were Scotland's most feared strikers.

The shrewd Smith had made it four-in-a-row – nine points clear of second-placed Hearts – and the Scottish Cup was back at Ibrox for the first time in 11 years.

Walter forms old pals' pact

WALTER SMITH had the job of his dreams but, as the new season got underway, there was little time to sit back and dwell on fulfilling a lifetime's ambition. The Gaffer had work to do and, as he faced the daunting challenge of reshaping Rangers, he had a trusted ally beside him. A friendship spanning more than 20 years bonds Smith and Archie Knox, yet the manager feared he had no chance of tempting his old pal away from Manchester United.

He recalled: "We were always on the phone to each other and stayed in touch, but he'd been a success everywhere and now he was with Alex Ferguson at Manchester United.

"I didn't think I'd get him, but I called and he said he'd be interested

NET GAIN... Andy Goram was Walter Smith's first major signing and can surely be classed as one of his best

and that was all the encouragement I needed.

"It was my first managerial job and, although I'd been a coach for 13 years, it was tough at times.

"Archie had been a manager in his own right and securing his help was vital."

Smith and Knox had played together in the Dundee United side that lost 3-0 to Celtic in the Scottish Cup Final of 1974.

As their playing careers ended, their love of coaching drew them into hours of discussions on the game.

Smith continued learning under Jim McLean at Tannadice, while Knox went off on his travels.

And Walter smiled "He'd gone to be a manager at Forfar where I remembered him running Rangers close in a League Cup semi-final one night, much to my disgust!

"He then went to Aberdeen as No.2 and we crossed swords in the New Firm derbies before he went off to boss Dundee.

"I recall in the first season that I came to Rangers that Hearts and Celtic were going for the title.

"Archie probably won't like reminding of this now, but he beat Hearts 2-0 on the last day of the season and handed the title to Celtic.

"We had to win our last game that season against Motherwell to get into Europe and pip Dundee – for me that shows you the job he did at Dens."

Now they were together at the head of a club still shrugging off the numbing shock of Souness's departure.

AND there were critical decisions to be made before the Ibrox curtain-raiser with St Johnstone on August 10.

"The biggest single factor that year was the three-foreigners rule coming in," stressed Smith.

"I knew 12 of my players were going to be ruled as foreigners in European ties.

"The title had been won, but the work had just started because in a three-month spell we sold eight players and brought in six.

"I knew at the beginning we wouldn't be at our strongest because this was basically a brand new team.

"It wasn't ideally what I'd have wanted, but now I look back and think that shake-up was the best thing that happened to us.

"It brought a real freshness to the place. Looking back, the three foreigners rule became a blessing in disguise for Rangers."

It was a frantic summer

'Goram is worth 15 to 20 points every season'

HOME GUARD…
Andy Goram
replaced
England's Chris
Woods in goal
as Rangers
complied with
the three
foreigner rule

as Smith paid Hibs £1m for Scotland No.1 Andy Goram and jettisoned England goalkeeper Chris Woods.

Six years on, that first major signing must surely be hailed as one of the club's best-ever deals.

Goram's brilliance in goal has been worth between 15 and 20 points a season to Rangers.

The departure of steady servants Stuart Munro and Tom Cowan made way for the buccaneering David Robertson – a £970,000 steal from Aberdeen – at left-back.

He was to fully justify his manager's faith and Smith said: "I always felt David had the potential to be an exciting player for Rangers. His level of consistency and play since he came here has been phenomenal."

Although Rangers couldn't resist £5.5m from Marseille for Trevor Steven, the disappointment of seeing the classy England international go was quickly quelled.

The manager had already splashed out £2.2m to bring Alexei Mikhailitchenko from Italian giants Sampdoria and he was

TO THE FOUR...
Rangers collect their fourth successive Championship trophy on the final day of the 1991/92 season

'There's no such thing as a hiding place at Rangers'

to shrug off the Steven sale by landing Scotland midfielder Stuart McCall from Everton 48 hours after Trev's last game.

So it was very much Smith's side that took to the field against Saints – and the traditionally slow starters got off to a flyer with a 6-0 win.

Mark Hateley rattled in a hat-trick, including a memorable, thumping header, Mo Johnston struck twice and

Ian Ferguson contributed with a solo goal.

Rangers were out of the blocks in style and, in midweek, Motherwell's gangling Dutch import Rob Maaskant unwittingly kept them on track with a stylish header past his own keeper.

Steven said "au revoir" to Rangers with a goal before jetting out to France.

Sadly, it was to turn into a nightmare of pay wrangles with the now-disgraced

Bernard Tapie at the Stade Velodrome before Trev – so often cursed with injuries in the seasons that have followed – returned to the Ibrox fold 11 months later.

He left a side in cruise control, but the wheels came off at Tynecastle as Scott Crabbe's speculative, dipping volley after just 40 seconds deceived Goram to give Hearts a shock 1-0 win.

The keeper carried the can but recovered to notch a

clean sheet in a 4-0 home win over Dunfermline before Gers made the short journey to Parkhead for the first Old Firm dust-up of the season on August 31.

Smith pointed out: "That Hearts defeat may have helped us in an odd way because it showed the new players something they had to learn – there's no such thing as a hiding place at Rangers. They'd lost the first away game of the season

and hadn't played all that badly but the criticism was fierce."

H E added: "I was nervous as I took my seat for the first match against Celtic as Rangers manager, but no more than I would be as a fan or assistant-boss.

"The only difference being a Rangers fan is it means that I know exactly what this game means to people – the dismay or pleasure it brings into their lives depending on the result.

"The truth is, nothing means more to each set of supporters than beating the other lot. That game was important because I wanted to prove to the Rangers fans that I could get results when it mattered."

Smith needn't have worried – the man AC Milan fans tagged Attila the Hun was back to his best.

Mark Hateley's battle to win over the Light Blue Legions had been won the day he clinched the title three months earlier.

Now he was on fire and, when the Celts' defence misjudged a McCall through-ball, he seared round Packie Bonner and slid home the opener with the backtrack-

ing Derek Whyte left clinging to the rigging like a drunken sailor.

After the break, a sweet piece of headed interplay with Johnston gave Hateley time and space to arrow in an another accurate drive. Bonner spilled it and it was party time for Rangers.

So they ended August on a high, but the Tynecastle slip meant Hearts and Aberdeen were still a point clear.

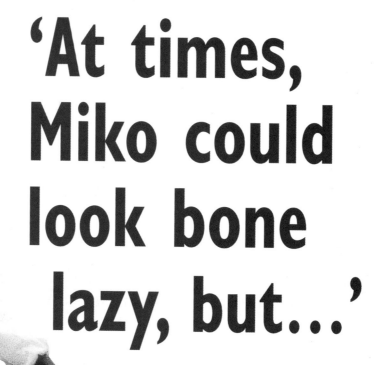

'At times, Miko could look bone lazy, but...'

GIFTED... but not every Rangers fan had as much time for Alexei Mikhailitchenko as his boss did

A Scott Nisbet goal – the cult hero was to nab five in 20 games that season – and a roaring strike from Pieter Huistra brought a 2-0 win at Falkirk.

But the game's shining moment came from the man who was to become one of the greatest Ibrox enigmas.

The merits of Alexei Mikhailitchenko used to spark heated debates on supporters' buses – costly waster or misunderstood genius?

For this writer, it was always the latter. Maverick Miko could look bone-lazy at times but he would then produce one killer pass, one clever turn or one piece of sublime vision that made him worth watching.

Smith, too, remains convinced of the Ukrainian's worth to Rangers, and has a piece of classic Alexei that still sticks in his mind from that day.

HE smiled: "He looked up and smacked a shot from 60 yards that flew just over with their keeper scrambling – and it wasn't the first time he'd tried a stunt like that.

"Mikhailitchenko was a terrific player but he never fitted into Scottish fans' perceptions of how their players should be.

"There wasn't enough running and tackling about him for some people and some say he was a failure. I'll never agree with that."

Alexei scored 10 goals in 24 starts in that championship season as Smith shared out his duties on the left with talented Dutchman Huistra.

Clearly, his manager will always have a special place in his heart for a player who always steadfastly refused to lump the ball anywhere.

Walter revealed: "He was a hugely popular signing in the dressing-room. The rest of the boys loved him and I had a great deal of time for him.

"The frustrating thing about Alexei was you felt he could show his quality more often.

"I'm not saying Mikhailitchenko was the greatest Rangers player ever, but he played his part.

"He was such a gifted man and he left here after five years with five championship medals."

Smith's former club,

IM-PRESS-IVE: Scott Nisbet became a fans' favourite – and a regular feature in the sports pages – with five goals in the 1991-92 season

A WORD IN YOUR YEAR... everyone wanted to speak to Ally about the massive part he played in making it four-in-a-row for Rangers

'McCoist was to thrive under Walter'

Dundee United, then held the champs to a 1-1 draw at Ibrox, with kid striker Duncan Ferguson grabbing their goal before Rangers flew out for a European Cup examination against Sparta in Prague.

Jiri Nemec's freak effort gave his side a slender win but, after the 1-0 defeat, an anxious Smith was having private doubts about his side's readiness for battle with the elite.

He recalled: "We didn't play too well and lost 1-0. I thought we weren't ready for that level.

"Yet we came back and beat them 2-1 at Ibrox, only to go out on away goals.

"Sparta went on to do very well in the Champions League and they beat Barcelona. They were a better team than I thought."

That second-leg sickener was the last act in an awful week for Smith, whose side had won 2-1 at St Mirren before seven days of woe.

First came the Skol Cup semi-final with Hibs and Rangers were rocked as Goram raced from his goal and punched clear at Hampden. The ball fell kindly for Mickey Weir and his cross beyond the keeper was perfect for Keith Wright to glance Rangers out.

Saturday brought more misery as goals from Brian Grant and Eoin Jess gave Aberdeen a 2-0 win at Ibrox.

Rangers then were on the ropes for the Sparta clash on their own turf but a marvellously courageous display and two goals from Stuart McCall had them through until it all blew up in their faces.

NISBET poked a leg at a harmless cross and somehow it crept beyond the reach of Goram.

With that Crabbe howler at Tynecastle still fresh in the memory banks, the team were now out of the Skol Cup and out of Europe – Andy was firmly cast as the

scapegoat. Smith's judgement in buying the former Hibs star was called into question but the manager never wavered.

He explained: "There are different pressures on goalkeepers at Rangers than anywhere else.

"I was looking for how he would react to errors as there's nothing you can do once the mistake has been made.

"Andy Goram's reaction to any setback is a grim determination to put it right. If Andy was an outfield player, he'd be a Dave Mackay or a Billy Bremner. He detests losing and that's why I never had any fears."

That was a soul searching time for the Rangers boss and, as he faced a testing October, there were big question marks

over his team. Ally McCoist provided the answers.

McCoist, benched and discarded by Souness as their uneasy relationship simmered, was to thrive under Smith.

His season began in earnest at Broomfield with a double in a 4-0 win over Airdrie, before he cemented a classic free-kick past John Burridge on the way to another two-goal haul in a 4-2 home win over Hibs.

Now he was on a roll and, once more, "McCoist (2)" went on the scoresheet after a 3-2 win at his old club, St Johnstone.

Another Super Ally strike and Miko's first for the club gave Rangers a 2-0 home win over Hearts before a poor 1-1 Ibrox draw with Falkirk.

A 3-2 defeat at Dundee United came hot on the heels of that.

But, as McCoist bagged yet another brace, the

'Dale Gordon shone in a debut you'd toil to script'

omens were there that he would not be content to accept second best.

He'd scored nine goals in six games in a hectic month and vindicated a belief in him which Smith had held since he sat in the Ibrox boot room with Souness calling the shots.

That Tannadice loss signalled the end of Maurice Johnston's Rangers career, two-and-a-half years after his bombshell signing from Nantes.

He went south to Everton and Smith placed his faith in the striker he'd always felt should be Rangers' first-choice No.9.

Walter said: "Graeme's preference was for Maurice Johnston and Mark Hateley but I'd always felt that, of the three of them, Ally McCoist was the most likely to score a goal.

"So that, allied to the fact that Mo has always moved around a lot in his career, framed my thinking.

"Johnston was an excellent player and so was big Mark but the man for me who would always get you the most goals was McCoist.

"When Everton came in for Mo the way was clear for me to see if I was right."

BY the time Celtic came calling on November 2, there was an inevitability about McCoist being the name on the scoresheet for Rangers.

However, the same couldn't be said for the source of the Hoops' goal.

Ally swooped to score with a glorious diving header from Gary Stevens' cross, but an uncharacteristic Nigel Spackman error undid Rangers. His backpass was sloppy and there was £1.1m Liam Brady misfit Tony Cascarino to score.

It was to be a rare day of joy for the player they called Can't-Scorino as he struggled to live up to his billing.

Rangers, though, had let another vital point slip.

Fortunately, there were to be no such mistakes when a new star took his first bow at East End Park, Dunfermline, a week later.

Dale Gordon arrived from Norwich City and shone in a debut that you'd toil to script, scoring two and terrorising the Pars in a 5-0 hammering.

Smith looked on delighted, but confessed: "In this amazing first 25 minutes I thought he was a different player from the one I'd bought!

"Seriously, he came to the club with his reputation

DISCO FEVER... Dale Gordon in action and (above right) scoring against Dunfermline on his debut for Rangers

as Disco Dale, the winger with the shuffle, but he was really a working player. He was to put in some great shifts for us and I'll never forget how hard he grafted to help us beat Leeds 2-1 away in the European Cup the following season."

Now Rangers were back in the groove and Hateley and McCoist were wreaking havoc, plundering all the goals as Airdrie were whipped 4-0 and Hibs humbled 3-0 at Easter Road.

But another shocker was waiting in the shape of toiling St Mirren, who were to surrender their Premier League status that season.

Kevin McGowne's goal stunned the home fans into silence and once more Smith's side were staring at a three-point deficit between them and pace-setters Hearts.

Gordon and Gough got the goals to cure the hang-

over against Motherwell before one of the games of the season produced three of the best goals any travelling Rangers fan could wish to witness.

The venue was Pittodrie on December 4 and the Mark and Ally Show came to town – big time.

First, Gordon saw a volley brilliantly stopped by Theo Snelders, but Hateley simply rattled the ball back beyond the Dutchman from 18 yards.

Then Attila left David Winnie staggering in his wake, like a man vainly chasing a bus, before ripping a shot home for his second after a sweeping move that he'd started way back in his own half.

Goals from Brian Irvine and Theo ten Caat kept the Dons in the hunt, but McCoist produced the cutest of chips with his left foot to seal a 3-2 win and

'Smith knew he'd found the strikers he wanted'

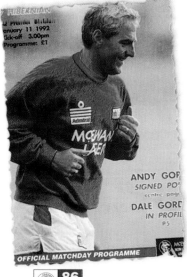

Smith knew for sure now that he'd found the strikers he wanted.

He recalled: "An incredible partnership began to form. Hateley and McCoist had a double act that you will struggle to see bettered at this club.

"They went on to score 55 league goals between them that season and they were remarkable."

That night was to prove significant, as it was over three months and 15 league games before the Light Blues tasted defeat again.

Hateley stayed on the goal trail in successive 3-1 wins against St Johnstone and Falkirk before the team triumphed again in front of the new face of Ibrox.

Almost a year-and-a-half after construction began, the £20m Club Deck of the Main Stand was opened on December 21 to allow another 7,169 Gers fanatics to see the title action.

A crowd of 45,407 crammed in to witness a familiar star in a familiar role as McCoist nabbed both in a 2-0 win against Dundee

United. Then goals from Stevens and Gordon dumped Dunfermline 2-1 to end the month on a high.

After five months of his first full campaign Smith was quietly satisfied.

He said: "After losing out to Hibs, Aberdeen and Sparta in that one week there had been big question marks over everything, but we settled down.

"After that, the team were exceptional. I think it all started in that bedding-in period in late 1991.

"I knew there would be

teething problems but they got to know each other and that dogged resistance to defeat began to grow.

"We weren't the best footballing team, but no-one went for a stroll-about – this was a working side.

"But I had the feeling they could be something special and so it proved."

Ne'erday brought the traditional Old Firm derby, this time at Parkhead, and a goal that will live long in the fans' memories and forever in the scorer's.

McCoist's typically

predatory strike had been levelled by a bulleting header from Englishman Tony Mowbray, before streetwise Ally conned goalkeeper Gordon Marshall into making the challenge that brought a penalty.

The nerveless Hateley scored and the scene was set for Bomber to go in and finish the job. John Brown's commitment to the Ibrox cause has never been questioned by anyone who wants their head to stay on their shoulders.

That's why you'll seldom

see an explosion of joy like the sub produced that day, after he'd been allowed to stroll onto his favoured left foot and rifle the ball in off the post from 20 yards.

Brown was off and running and Smith laughed: "I'll always remember him hurdling the hoardings at the Rangers end and cavorting around.

"If it had been 1997, he'd probably have been sent off for those type of antics, but it was just a case of one Rangers fan fulfilling the dream that every single

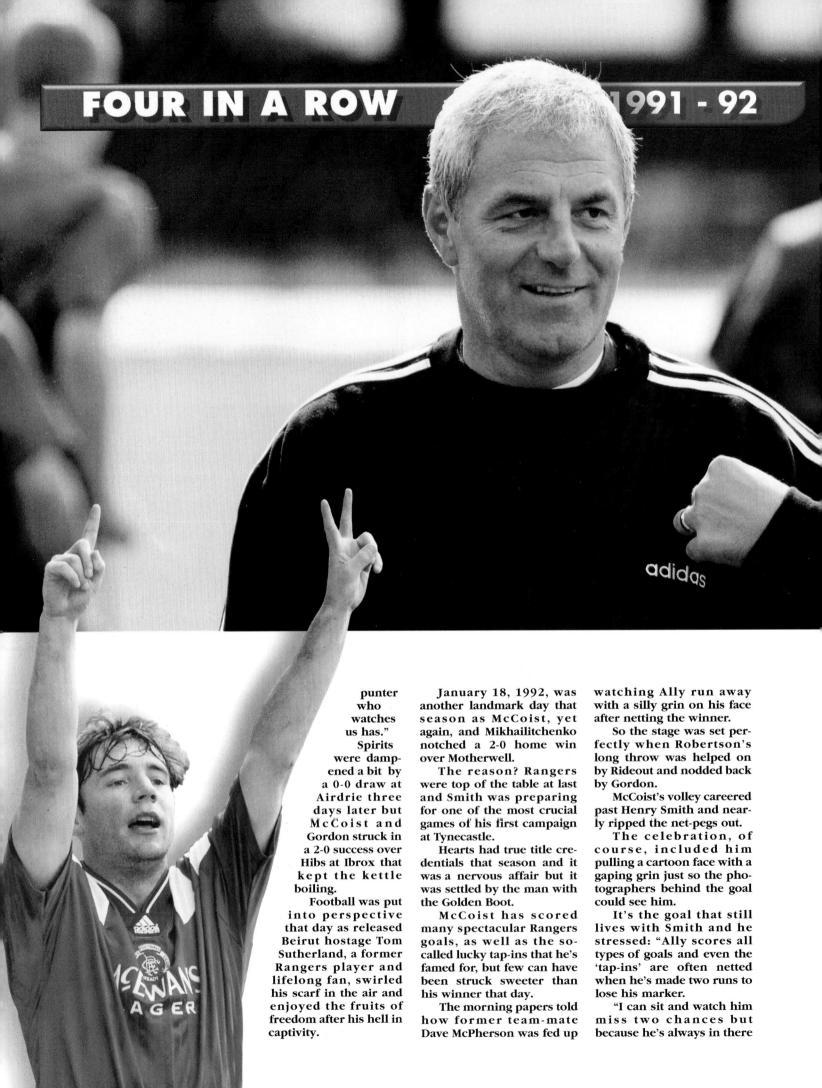

punter who watches us has." Spirits were dampened a bit by a 0-0 draw at Airdrie three days later but McCoist and Gordon struck in a 2-0 success over Hibs at Ibrox that kept the kettle boiling.

Football was put into perspective that day as released Beirut hostage Tom Sutherland, a former Rangers player and lifelong fan, swirled his scarf in the air and enjoyed the fruits of freedom after his hell in captivity.

January 18, 1992, was another landmark day that season as McCoist, yet again, and Mikhailitchenko notched a 2-0 home win over Motherwell.

The reason? Rangers were top of the table at last and Smith was preparing for one of the most crucial games of his first campaign at Tynecastle.

Hearts had true title credentials that season and it was a nervous affair but it was settled by the man with the Golden Boot.

McCoist has scored many spectacular Rangers goals, as well as the so-called lucky tap-ins that he's famed for, but few can have been struck sweeter than his winner that day.

The morning papers told how former team-mate Dave McPherson was fed up

watching Ally run away with a silly grin on his face after netting the winner.

So the stage was set perfectly when Robertson's long throw was helped on by Rideout and nodded back by Gordon.

McCoist's volley careered past Henry Smith and nearly ripped the net-pegs out.

The celebration, of course, included him pulling a cartoon face with a gaping grin just so the photographers behind the goal could see him.

It's the goal that still lives with Smith and he stressed: "Ally scores all types of goals and even the 'tap-ins' are often netted when he's made two runs to lose his marker.

"I can sit and watch him miss two chances but because he's always in there

'Rangers had the scent of victory'

I know he'll net the third, that's the best."

Yet another side of the McCoist armoury was used to shoot down St Mirren in the next match, when he slickly switched the ball from the right to left in one movement to evade Les Fridge and guide a classic into the corner before Mikhailitchenko tied it up at 2-1.

By now, chairman David Murray's business acumen was biting into every aspect of the club and this was to be the last season they played in Admiral kit.

A new, lavish, five-year deal was signed with Adidas and the strip was to make its debut in that season's Tennents Scottish Cup Final.

But commercial clout off the field is driven by success on it and, although a 0-0 home draw with Aberdeen was a setback, Hateley helped himself to a hat-trick in a 5-0 win over Airdrie.

All of a sudden, Hearts were wilting and Rangers were seven points clear at the end of February – the champions had the scent of victory once more.

Hibs were seen off 3-1 before Nisbet, a bag of eccentricities and whole-heartedness who had become such a favourite, scored his final goal of the season with a header in a 3-1 win at Dunfermline.

His cult status and a bizarre Champions League fluke against FC Bruges the following season often overshadowed the fact that Nissy was a very capable player.

A disgruntled Souness once tossed a Rothman's Football Yearbook at him and said: "Find yourself a club in there."

But he stuck it out and Smith and his backroom staff were dejected when a pelvic injury forced him to quit at the age of just 25.

Walter said: "He was simply delighted to be playing for Rangers.

"He played right-back, centre-half and even striker for us and that's vital."

Rangers went into the final Old Firm league clash bombing, but were blitzed by fired-up Celtic, who took the points thanks to goals from Charlie Nicholas and Gerry Creaney.

Ten days later, however, the men who had been humbled put in a Hampden performance that was more than enough to restore their dented pride.

A tough league match had to be negotiated at St Johnstone before that though and, in a game that saw Ian Durrant's first start for five months, they did it at a costly price.

Unlucky ex-Rangers keeper Lindsay Hamilton saved a spot-kick from Hateley only to see the big man gobble up the rebound before winning it with a towering header.

'Durrant, the heart of Ibrox'

The downside was a back injury in the dying seconds that put him out of the midweek semi with Rangers' bitterest rivals.

Now primarily, this book is a tale of a club a league apart – the story of champions making history.

But Walter Smith would never let it go on the shelves without telling the tale of March 31, 1992 – the night he believes sums up what Rangers are all about.

The Tennents Scottish Cup semi-final that night was played in driving rain and Rangers looked like drowning when Robertson whacked into Joe Miller and was controversially ordered off by ref Andrew Waddell.

Rangers now faced 84 minutes with just ten men. It looked an impossible task, but they clung on and, as the break loomed, McCoist swept home what was to prove to be the winner.

For Smith, it wasn't just the passage to the final, it was the route to showing once and for all that he was not the leader of a band of cold-eyed, footballing mercenaries.

He insisted: "That night was not the work of players who cared only about the money as I'd heard said so many times.

"It was as good as I have been involved in – they stuck together, gritted their teeth and fought for the badge on the jerseys.

"It had nothing to do with money. It was all about pride and playing for Rangers.

"That was the performance that really brought the Cup back to Ibrox for the first time in 11 years and no team could have turned in a grittier 90 minutes.

"That was the night I truly felt they could go on and on winning and they did."

It was fitting that, on a night that will go down in the books as one of their best ever when the club celebrates its 125th birthday in 1998, Durrant should be at the heart of it.

Much has been said and much written about that fateful afternoon at Pittodrie on October 8, 1988 when the red mist came down over Aberdeen's Neil Simpson.

It was a moment of madness that may well have ruined Simpson's career. It certainly

threatened to wreck Durrant's.

The saddest thing is we'll never know how good Ian could have been. It's to his credit he ever came back at all after the surgery that has left his knee looking like a roadmap.

Smith shares the regret and he said: "I've never been involved with another player as naturally gifted as Ian Durrant.

"When I came to the club at first I could see that he did everything like it was second nature.

"He had great fitness, he was a decent tackler and on the ball he was different class.

"He had the touches and then when he got himself into the box he was a really good finisher.

"So when that happened to him it was a bitter disappointment but then that season we had him back at last.

"It would have been difficult for anyone to come back and reach those levels again after all he had

been through. But he came back to be a really important player in the squad and I'm still delighted he's been a part of us for so long."

Durrant helped the team to a 4-1 win over Falkirk on April 7, with his great pal McCoist grabbing a hat-trick as the title beckoned.

Another long-term absentee made a rare appearance that day.

But you won't find the same admiration in Walter Smith's heart for Oleg Kuznetsov.

The Russian defender goes down in the book of many as one who was stolen from the club by the cruel hand of fate when he twisted awkwardly on the McDiarmid Park turf and badly injured his knee.

But Smith revealed: "Kuznetsov had played against us for Dynamo Kiev and Graeme was delighted to get him in 1990, especially

when he had such a brilliant debut in a 5-0 win over St Mirren.

"In the next game against St Johnstone he injured his knee and was out for a year.

"For me, he never really showed the determination to come back from that in the way he should have done.

"I don't like to criticise players but he didn't show the right approach."

Four-in-a-row was now within touching distance and an Alexei opener at Tannadice brought the 91st Rangers league goal of the season to break the Premier scoring record.

Jim McInally levelled but Brown thumped home a right foot drive to set up a title-clinching party at home to St Mirren on April 18.

McCoist poked the ball under Campbell Money and gleefully stabbed home.

Then Chris

Vinnicombe and Mikhailitchenko set up Stevens before McCoist and Huistra wrapped it up.

Smith's side popped the champagne corks on a season that was to see them score 101 league goals and lose just five times in 44 games.

They were the champions and they showed their professionalism by winning 2-1 at Motherwell and drawing at home to Hearts.

A 2-0 win at Aberdeen was the icing on the cake. McCoist scored both to take his league haul for the season to 34.

A Scottish Cup final victory over Airdrie meant the double and the Smith Era had started in earnest.

Walter pointed out: "That team was to win seven consecutive Scottish trophies and go 12 European games without defeat.

"They were also to go on a 44-game unbeaten run the next season and had pride to match their ability.

"I consider them the benchmark for Rangers teams of the future. Any team that wants to emulate them will have a lot to live up to."

FIVE IN A ROW
Scottish Premier D

This chapter is brought to you
in association with

YEARS from now when they talk about the true Rangers greats they will look back in awe at this team. The team that won the Treble, the team that went 44 games unbeaten in all competitions, the team that never lost a match in Europe and went within an ace of the Champions Cup Final.

There are times in the lifetime of a football club when one play-er will hit the highest peak of his form but seldom can so many have achieved greatness in one season.

From Player of the Year Andy Goram through the sheer grit of John Brown in defence, Stuart McCall in midfield and 49-goal Ally McCoist up front this was a team in their prime.

Trevor Steven and Dave McPherson both returned for sec-ond stints at Ibrox, it was to be the best decision they had ever made.

Ally: The year of cheers and tears

THE picture of a season, the end of a move that took your breath away and the diving header that buried England's champions – it was the goal of Ally McCoist's life.

Rangers had won the Battle of Britain against Leeds United and the game's premier penalty box predator had struck home and away to send his side into the Champions League.

Flick away from that joy-filled image to the face of famed boozer Oliver Reed, grafted on to a cardboard cut-out of Ally and emblazoned with a title-winning message RIGHT BOYS, LET'S

PARTY! Whether Olly could have handled a night out with the Rangers first team squad is up for debate. But at least he was upright this time, strapped to the crocked McCoist's back as the striker hobbled round Ibrox on crutches celebrating five in a row.

Ally had broken his leg in Scotland's 5-0 humbling by Portugal and would miss the clinching of his club's first Treble in 15 years.

He went through the emotional wringer yet he confesses that a season he ended heartbroken and in plaster will always remain the BEST of his life.

He recalled: "As I flew home from Portugal I knew then that

the season of my dreams was over, the team were going for the Treble and I wouldn't be there.

"I was devastated and I could lie and say all I wanted to do was just be there when we won the Treble.

"That would be wrong – I wanted to play and behind the smiles it was bittersweet.

"Yet now as I look back at the records of that season it frightens me, I played in the best team of my life."

It had all started on August 1 against McCoist's former club St Johnstone and what was to be a momentous campaign began in scrappy fashion.

With the fans fearing a goalless

draw on the opening day McCoist swooped to force the winner past Andy Rhodes from close range.

And he pointed out: "As is so often the case when the adrenaline is pumping so much it was a nervous start and we have always been notoriously slow out the blocks in any case.

"But Goughie's knockdown put me in the frame and I was just glad to score – we were off and running."

A 2-0 win over Airdrie and a goalless draw at Hibs followed before Rangers were left punch-drunk by a stunning 4-3 reverse at the hands of newly-promoted Dundee.

Simon Stainrod strode the Dens Park touchline clad in a flowing raincoat and black fedora, whipping his side into a frenzy as a double from Billy Dodds and goals by Ian Gilzean and Ivo den Bieman secured a famous victory.

McCoist darted in at the near post to strike twice and Ian Ferguson rifled in a belter but Rangers went down.

Yet Ally stressed: "That loss at Dundee was to be the

'After Dundee Rangers didn't lose a game for SEVEN months'

catalyst for a 44-game unbeaten run.

"But there were two things that stuck in my throat after that defeat.

"First of all, Simon was very uncomplimentary towards Rangers, basically saying we beat teams only because they were scared of us.

"He suggested that all you had to do was go for Rangers' jugular and you would beat them – well a few teams were to try that season and come off worse.

"Secondly – and perhaps even more serious – Simon was strutting around in a fedora and he was credited with bringing the hat back into Scottish football fashion.

"Anyone with any sense knows it was McCoist who did that with my superb Crocodile Dundee number at Tannadice a few years earlier!"

The date of the Dens demise was worth noting – August 15, 1992. Rangers would not lose another match in any competition for SEVEN MONTHS.

Yet the surrender at Dundee had hardly been the

ideal preparation for the first Old Firm clash of the season at Ibrox.

Trevor Steven was back in Rangers' starting line-up after his dream £5.5million move to Marseille ended in recriminations and bitter disputes over wages.

Back home all the gifted Englishman had to worry about was football and against Celtic

Trevor's ever-ticking football brain took him into space to accept a Mark Hateley lay-off and thunder a shot low past Gordon Marshall.

He wheeled away to celebrate but the offside flag wrongly silenced the screams of delirium from the packed stands.

Then Gerry Creaney smashed Celtic ahead and Rangers were in the mire. The rescue mission was headed by an Old Firm talisman.

Ian Durrant lives for big

'Ian and Ally could tear any defence to shreds'

games, whether it's Europe or a clash with Celtic he relishes it. Throughout his career he has been the definition of a big-game player.

So it proved again when Pieter Huistra's pace took him to the byeline and the cross was prodded back by Hateley for a shot that sub Ian exploded into the top corner.

A thrilling goal but only a point, and a week later Walter Smith's side were toiling again when Aberdeen's Roy Aitken bulleted home a volley to send the home fans reaching for the valium.

Rangers trailed at the break to the nearest challengers – they'd eventually top by nine points but then they produced 45 minutes of football that

were sprinkled with magic and laced with goals to savour.

Durrant curled home the first then sent McCoist racing clear to guide the second round Theo Snelders before Alexei Mikhailitchenko's lethal left foot clubbed home a half-volley for the clincher in a 3-1 triumph.

Durrant and McCoist are the kings of the dressing-room one-liners, at the heart of every prank that keeps a smile on the face of Scotland's champions.

But when they play together, football remains a deadly serious business and at the height of their powers there was an almost telepathic understanding that could tear any defence to shreds. McCoist's

BLUES BROTHERS...
McCoist and Durrant have
been two of the
mainstays of Rangers'
9-year title domination and
Trevor Steven, right, enjoyed
two spells at Ibrox

strike that day was a stunning example as Durrant smuggled the ball clear in midfield and watched Ally bend his run across the very edges of the Dons' offside trap.

The spearing pass was precision played, McCoist sped through to clip in a classic and he said: "There has been no other midfielder who knew my game so well.

"I could make runs blind and Ian would deliver the ball right into my path.

"But in one reckless tackle from Aberdeen's Neil Simpson all that was so nearly snatched away for good – it was a horrendous injury.

"He did well to come back at all, yet in that Champions League season he was once again one of our best players.

"Who knows how he would have developed and how far he would have gone without that injury? I doubt if we'll see his like again."

McCoist then walked out of Fir Park with the first of three match balls he'd land for league hat-tricks that season.

And the third in a 4-1 win was typical of the barefaced cheek of a striker who has always managed to play with a smile on his face.

He recalled: "It was a tap-in I knew I was going to score and I can remember letting their keeper, Billy Thomson, catch up with me and teasing him before I put it in. I have

'Rangers won 4-0 and Ally hit the lot'

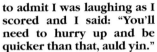

to admit I was laughing as I scored and I said: "You'll need to hurry up and be quicker than that, auld yin."

"A bit harsh perhaps but when he later signed for us I told him I didn't count that as a hat-trick because it was too easy to score against him.

"I've always been good at building up other players' confidence like that."

Rangers repeated the 4-1 scoreline at Partick Thistle in a game that produced memorable goals from Gough — switching from his left to volley home a blistering right-foot shot — and Hateley.

Big Mark deserved full marks for vision in attempting to score from 45 yards but Jags keeper Craig Nelson will try to hide the video of this one from his children in years to come.

A 2-0 win over Hearts then sent Rangers into the Skol Cup semi-final with St Johnstone at Hampden and once more McCoist bit the hand that used to feed him with a hat-trick in a comfortable 3-1 win.

Aberdeen were waiting in the Final but Rangers had league business to attend to and a trip to Tannadice brought one of the proudest days in the life of Ally McCoist MBE. With Gough

injured, boss Smith went to his striker's hotel room and broke the news that he would lead out the team the following day.

The fan who'd been in love with the club since the days when he won a Light Blues strip in a newspaper competition was captain of Rangers.

To cap it all his side chose September 26 to serve up one of their best away days of the season ...

A Huistra double and a Steven header added to stand-in skipper Ally's customary strike racked up a 4-0 win.

McCoist's life has always read like a comic book tale and the following week it got even better as he kept the armband in a 4-0 Ibrox win over Falkirk — and scored the lot.

He grabbed the first with a volley while he was lying on his backside in the box.

He said: "The four goals I scored that day gave me an unbelievable high, my best ever haul in a game for Rangers and it all happened when I was captain.

"I seemed to keep finding the positions that season and every time I arrived on a run into the box my mates would find me.

"Those goals came in a run that brought me 12

goals in six games and I'll never forget that.

"The best scoring run I had before that was 11 goals in seven games — for the Boys Brigade!"

Lucky, it's the one word you always hear associated with McCoist but it masks the truth of his skills as a striker.

It was a LUCKY rebound, he was LUCKY to score there – its nonsense.

Slow down the video tape of his goals in the first leg of the Battle of Britain against Leeds that season and you're given a cameo of the art of scoring.

AT first glance you might think he simply arrives to prod the ball home after John Lukic parries Dave McPherson's fizzing header.

In reality he darts into two clever runs, changing direction to lose his marker and find a yard to gamble on the ricochet that brought him a priceless goal.

The joker-in-the-pack public person is only half the story.

Behind it there is a striker who worked so hard to make himself better and overcame stinging abuse from the fans that would have sent less courageous players scurrying for the Ibrox exit door.

In the next league clash at St Johnstone Rangers were rampant, dismantling dejected Saints 5-1 with McCoist and partner in crime Hateley both netting doubles.

Ally had seen off a host of strikers in six years at Rangers before Souness brought Mo Johnston to Ibrox in 1989, his arrival changed things for good.

McCoist reflected: "Mark and Mo were the two players I was MADE to partner.

"I only really had the one full season with Mo but he was always the one I had wanted to play beside before Hateley emerged.

"I was personally delighted when Rangers signed Maurice but ironically he eventually put me on the bench.

"It wasn't right that the fans blamed Mark for that because in Graeme Souness' thinking it was Hateley and A.N. Other.

"So I sat it out but when Walter Smith put Mark and me together it just clicked right away – he was so good for me.

"We scored more than 140 goals in two seasons and I actually began to feel we were unstoppable. If one of us had an off day and didn't score, we KNEW the other would hit the target."

So it proved when Hibs visited Ibrox and Ally stepped off the bench to net a crucial winner just four days before the first leg of that 2-1 European Cup first leg win over Leeds United that is examined in greater depth later in this chapter.

Yet that Hibees game was tinged with tears – a minute's silence marked the first home match since the death of the legendary Willie Waddell who had served the club for 44 years and guided them to European Cup-Winners success over Moscow Dynamo

in 1972. Now the challenges were coming thick and fast but still Gers rose to them and the first trophy of the season was secured on October 25 at Hampden after a dramatic Skol Cup Final.

The new backpass law bamboozled Aberdeen keeper Snelders as he chested a David Winnie backpass right into the path of Stuart McCall who slotted home the opener.

Dons' Duncan Shearer swivelled to volley home a brilliant equaliser but Smith's side tied it all up in the cruellest of fashions.

The influential David Robertson angled over a treacherous cross from the left and Gary Smith could only watch in despair as his attempt at a header flew past his own keeper.

SIX days later Rangers mauled Motherwell 4-2 at Ibrox with another hat-trick from McCoist and a searing volley from one of the season's great success stories, John Brown.

It paved the way for a date with destiny at Elland Road where an unforgettable Hateley strike and McCoist's thrilling header left an army of English critics choking on their humble pie.

Victory was vindication for Smith and the team he'd built and stuffing the Auld Enemy's champions on their own turf sparked a rare midweek party for the Ibrox stars.

Ally grinned: "I will always remember the Thursday morning at our hotel in Leeds when the Gaffer got up a little the worse for wear and came down to the foyer.

"There sat Durranty and Stuart McCall in the bar and McCall, a Leeds fan as a kid, in his element after beating his heroes twice.

"He was still sipping champers and puffing on the largest Havana you've ever seen.

"Walter rubbed his bleary eyes and said sarcastically 'What do you reckon boys, do you think we should perhaps stop as we do have a game on Saturday'.

"McCall looked back deadpan and said 'Aw, come on boss it's only Celtic'."

After just 48 hours of rest Smith's men were back down off cloud nine and into the thick of the fray at Parkhead

'An army of English critics were choking on humble pie'

and once more they came up with the answers.

It was a 1-0 win brought about by Durrant's goal but built on Andy Goram's bullish defiance – he refused to beaten.

If a stop from Dariusz Wdowczyk's free-kick was breathtaking then his fingertip save from Stuart Slater's screamer beggared belief.

He sapped the life from Celtic and Durrant killed them stone dead when Dale Gordon's cross found McCoist at the back post for an unselfish header back to the feet of his trusted sidekick.

THE goal against their most bitter rivals, as ever, meant so much to the Ibrox double act. Ally said: "Durrant and I will always have a special bond because the day we stop playing for Rangers we'll probably end up sitting in the same section at Ibrox leading the choir.

"His injury remains one of the saddest things that has happened in my football career. But that goal was a flash of why he was so unique, he had that ability to spurt away from

defences and score goals." McCoist the provider was on the hunt for goals with a double in a 3-1 home win over Dundee and the counter that won a point at Hearts.

But injury was to rule him out of the Champions League opener with Marseille to allow deputy Gary McSwegan a rare chance to inspire one of Rangers' greatest ever comebacks in a 2-2 draw.

Three days later McSwegan was still on a high, rising to net a superb header in a 3-0 Ibrox win over Partick Thistle. The form had to dip somewhere and it came at Broomfield when only Brown's strike separated Rangers from defeat.

But after a 1-0 Euro win over CSKA Moscow in Bochum, McCoist bounced back to league action at Falkirk and his goal in a 2-1 win that day – a sweet, curling shot from 20 yards rubbished suggestions that he was purely a penalty box player.

This was without question a striker in his prime and the dismal days when he appeared to have no future under Souness seemed a million miles away. McCoist is not one to dwell on past hurt but when you look back on his glittering career it's crystal clear that the way he

'We had lost twice to Celtic and I was made the scapegoat'

was treated back then still rankles. He confessed: "There were times during my spells on the bench under Souness when it all got to me.

"When you're used to playing every week it's hard to accept that it has been taken away. The lowest ebb came when I was disciplined for going to Cheltenham races on my day off.

"I hadn't turned up late and I hadn't missed training. I hadn't felt I needed permission for my trip. I was being carpeted because what I did on my day off got up his nose and that hurt."

Behind the smiles there is steel. Remember this is a player who was left slumped in the dressing room, in tears as furious fans chanted for McCoist to go after a disastrous Scottish Cup defeat from Dundee in 1985.

Lesser men would have fled, instead he stayed and became the super Ally the fans love and adore today.

If he was ever going to quit Rangers it would have happened that day in March 1991 and he recalled: "I was forced to appear in front of the Press and it came out as 'Ally says sorry' but look back to the wording of my statement.

"If you do you'll find it read that in the manager's opinion I had breached discipline. Those were the key words because, if I'm honest, we'd just suffered two defeats from Celtic and I felt I was being cast as the scapegoat.

Under Smith, though, Ally had

flourished into one of the most feared strikers in Europe. And although he drew a rare blank in a 2-0 win over St Johnstone that brought goals from Robertson and Gough, Coisty was quickly back on target in a 3-2 Boxing Day revenge mission win at Dundee.

THAT sent the champs into the New Year clash with Celtic at Ibrox coursing with confidence. And once more when the chips were down Rangers had the right hand, Ferguson crossing for Hateley's experience to guide a header across goal and Steven swooping to nod home.

Two thrilling wins – 3-2 at home to Dundee United and 4-3 away to Hibs – kept Rangers on track and behind the scenes McCoist valued the camaraderie that had built up through a hectic season.

He recalled: "With so many games we seemed to be constantly on the move that season.

"And perhaps because of our great friendship and the fact that we never shut up, Durranty and I have roomed together in hotels all over the world.

"He started out at Rangers cleaning my boots and he has been a useful servant ever since. A fantastic tea-boy, he can also be relied upon to take messages and phone numbers in his role as my secretary."

But when injury or loss of form put Durrant out of the picture McCoist's routine was ditched. And he groaned: "Sharing with Ian is far easier than say John Brown who I am scared of.

"The remote control in a footballers' hotel room is a prized possession as you channel hop and while away the hours before a game.

"When I tried to take it off Bomber on one tip I soon discovered why they call him Hannibal Lecter, he actually GROWLED at me.

"Back on the road Rangers travelled to Pittodrie on February 2 for a game that

'When Goram finally spilled a shot it stuck on the line'

was critical to their championship hopes. They were to commit an act of robbery and take full points on the back of another goalkeeping masterclass from Goram. The Dons murdered Rangers that night, blitzing in shots from every angle.

But every time the home fans leapt to hail a goal, Goram defied them with another sickening stop. A fingertip save from Scott Booth was marvellous, an instinctive block when he must have only seen the blur of an Eoin Jess volley miraculous.

And Hateley twisted the knife with a trademark 16 yard header from Gary Stevens' cross before a second-half onslaught. Rangers survived the lot and when Goram finally did spill a shot, allowing Jess' effort to slip from his grasp and through his legs, the ball stuck on the line.

The keeper scooped it up and walked off a hero – his club were on the home straight towards another title.

Afterwards Goram was to pay tribute to a little-known figure behind the scenes. Alan Hodgkinson is the goalkeepers' guru, a gritty Yorkshireman who has made a science of clean sheets. He

first crossed swords with Goram at Oldham and after two weeks Andy hated the sight of him.

He couldn't understand what his coach was driving at – then it clicked and the pair are now inseparable.

Hodgkinson also helps out with Scotland and trains Everton's Neville Southhall and Manchester United superstar Peter Schmeichel but Goram is special.

The Rangers keeper insists Hodgy is his father figure, the man who took over when his dad, Lewis, died and the partnership has turned Andy into the keeper I rate as Europe's best.

Remarkably, McCoist failed to find the target in Rangers' next match despite a 5-0 scoreline against Falkirk that included another strike from marauding left-back David Robertson.

DRAWS with Airdrie and Dundee United then preceded a show of intent at Fir Park with Motherwell blitzed 4-0 as Mikhailitchenko ended a sparking afternoon with the cheekiest of goals through Sieb Dykstra's legs.

Now there had to be jaded legs in a dressing room where players were being asked to peak for big games every three days but still McCall had the quickness of thought to catch Hearts with a swift free-kick that

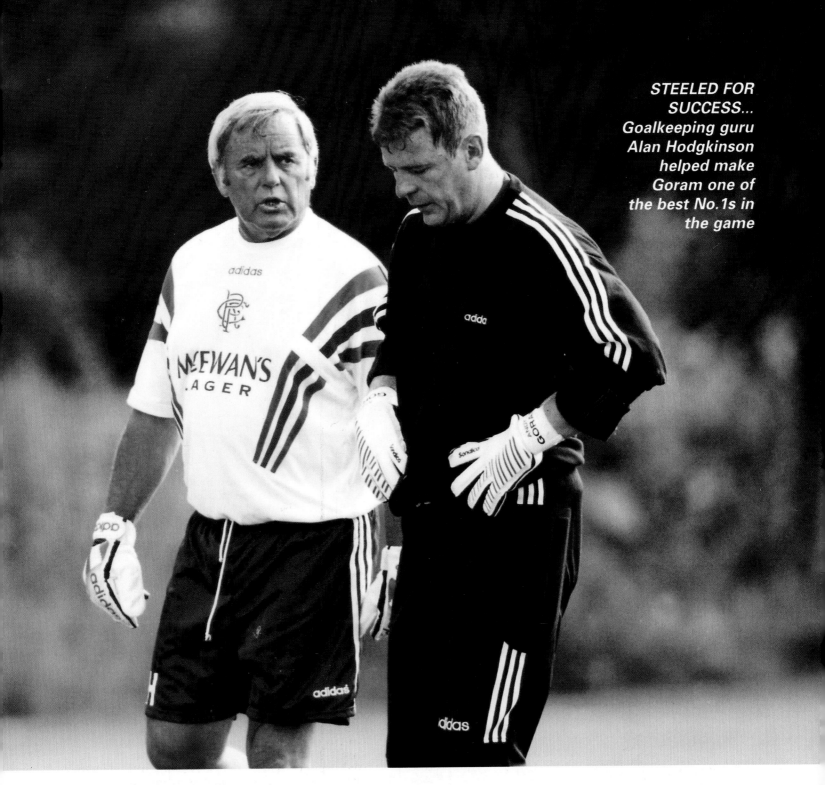

Robbo drilled home to set up a 2-1 win before the Champions League trip to Bruges.

Huistra clinched a point there and back home a 1-1 draw at Perth was the signal for Smith to give some of his young guns a shot against Hibs at Ibrox on March 13.

The club had raised Neil Murray, Steven Pressley and David Hagen to cope with the big occasion and they were to prove they could live at any level that season.

Hagen was the goalscoring hero this time, lofting the ball over Joe Tortolano before providing the coolest of finishes in a 3-0 win.

That put the club in good heart for a dramatic return against Bruges and the Saturday rest proved the tonic for the stars as Scott Nisbet's outrageous fluke gleaned a 2-1 success for 10-man Rangers following Hateley's red-card.

But it all has to end somewhere and that unbelievable, unbeaten run finally ground to a halt at Parkhead as the team ran out of steam and went down 2-1 to Celtic. Hateley netted for Rangers but goals by John Collins and Andy Payton won it for the Hoops in what was to be injury-stricken Nisbet's last game for Rangers.

It was over but what an experience it was – seven months of win bonuses and a lifetime full of memories.

McCoist reflected: "You milk those times dry and try and forget the bad days. It was a long way from the day early in my Rangers career when Jock Wallace told me Cardiff were after me and I could speak to them if I wanted.

"But whatever happened back then I never lost the belief that I could do it for Rangers.

"That season was the payback for all of the bad times rolled into one."

Rangers' only reaction to defeat was to dust themselves down and go gunning for more victories.

And they got them in the next two league matches, dumping Dundee and then winning a vital home clash with Aberdeen 2-0. Hateley beautifully teed up an Ian Ferguson special from 25

STOOKIE SHOT...
Ian Ferguson gives Ally a lift as the Ibrox men celebrate another title win

yards before heading into the path of McCoist who snapped up the second with a header that showed reflexes as razor sharp as they were on opening day.

Then came a quite bewildering week that summed up that remarkable season. It went like this.

DATE: Saturday, April 3, 1993.
VENUE: Parkhead.
OCCASION: Tennents Scottish Cup semi-final v Hearts.

Dave McPherson nets for Rangers and Allan Preston for Hearts before McCoist shows his bravery to lob the outrushing Nicky Walker for the winner.

The 49th goal of the season of his life is to be his last but Rangers, are through to the Final to face Aberdeen.

DATE: Wednesday, April 7, 1993.
VENUE: Stade Velodrome.
OCCASION: Champions League crunch v Marseille.

This was, in effect, a semi-final. Victory would have given Smith's side a place in the European Cup Final.

Franck Sauzee rifled the French in front before Durrant kept the dream alive with a whistling drive after Marseille's Basile Boli knocked out a Steven corner.

DATE: Saturday, April 10, 1993.
VENUE: Ibrox.
OCCASION: One step nearer the title v Motherwell.

Tired Rangers could easily have settled for a 0-0 draw. Instead they heap the pressure on and Brown fires an 86th minute winner.

Smith's men could have been forgiven for hitting the skids, instead

'Deep down I was hurting badly – it really did me in'

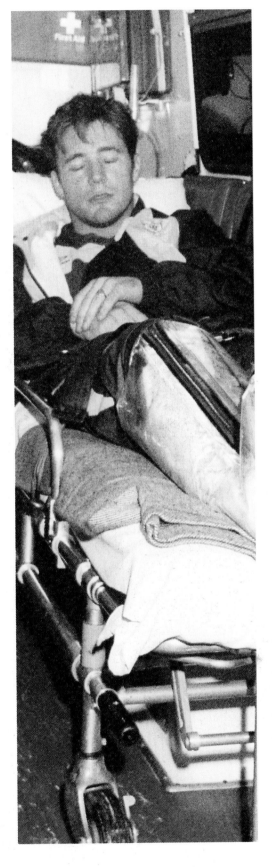

they carved out one of the goals of this or any other season in a 3-2 midweek win at Hearts. Durrant fed Hateley for a backheel to McCall and Stu deftly cut the ball across for big Mark to lob Nicky Walker with the cutest of headers.

Deputy striker McSwegan bagged a deadly double in a 3-1 win over Partick before the Euro prize agonisingly slipped away in a 0-0 draw with CSKA Moscow.

A WEEK later came the nightmare of Lisbon when McCoist broke his leg as Scotland were hammered 5-0 by Portugal. Boss Andy Roxburgh sighed: "A team died out there" – so did Ally's dream season.

It was also the end of Gough's tempestuous relationship with Roxburgh as he won the last of 61 caps and Ally winced: "I knew when I tried to get up that night in Lisbon that my leg was broken after Oceano's challenge.

"To be fair to him, I should have seen it coming – I actually kicked him in the act of shooting.

"Fernando Couto came in to swap jerseys after the game and ask how I was and that was a lovely gesture that consoled me a little."

But the master striker who had won two successive Golden Boots was finished for the season.

He was posted missing when the title was clinched at Airdrie on May 1 with a clever finish from McSwegan after a piercing pass from Hateley.

But Ferguson made sure McCoist took part in the celebrations, planting a cardboard cut-out Ally in the goalmouth

– it was later to return at Ibrox with Super Olly's head on it!

It was the first time the club had won five in a row for 62 years and with Mission Accomplished Rangers cruised through the last month, losing at Firhill and Pittodrie but winning against Dundee United and Falkirk before a two-week break in the run-up to the Cup Final against the Dons at Parkhead on May 29.

The experts said Rangers couldn't possibly lift themselves again – they had nothing left in the tank. The experts were wrong.

Murray put them in front with a shot that deflected off Brian Irvine before Hateley howitzered a thrilling goal past Snelders to make it 2-0 before the break.

Lee Richardson pulled one back but Rangers had done it – matching the feats of the Jock Wallace teams of 1976 and 1978.

An emotional McCoist hopped on to the Parkhead turf to embrace McPherson at the finish but the joy was tinged with a personal sadness.

He said: "I had 49 goals for Rangers that season and with eight games left I was dreaming of 50.

"I would have made it and then the broken leg ended it all on such a downer. The usual McCoist smile may have been presented to the outside world but deep down I was hurting badly– it really did me in.

"Sure, I had my second Golden Boot for consolation but there's something I can't explain about hitting 50. I just wanted it.

"It will remain one of the biggest regrets of my career that I didn't get there but I still had the time of my life trying."

PASSPORT TO GLORY

ONE more goal, just one more goal and Rangers would have faced the mighty AC Milan in the Champions Cup Final. Even four years on from the heady days of the magnificent 10-game unbeaten Euro run it's a sobering thought.

On March 7, 1993 Rangers travelled to Marseille in what was effectively the semi-final of the club game's most prestigious tournament.

Walter Smith's side were trailing to a strike from Franck Sauzee when a corner was knocked out to the edge of the box to Euro expert Ian Durrant.

What followed is etched on every Rangers fan's mind as the kid who grew up on the Ibrox terraces rifled an unstoppable, swerving half-volley into the far corner.

Rangers were almost there but it wasn't to be and Bernard Tapie's millionaires – later shamed and stripped of their crown in a match fixing scandal – got the win they needed in Bruges to make the Final.

Basile Boli's goal was to seal it for Marseille against Milan but Durrant still rues that away leg against the

'I've always felt Marseille were there for the taking'

French, believing the Scots had it in them to clinch one more crucial win.

He sighed: "I'll always regret Marseille, it was a great result but I felt they were there for the taking.

"I will maybe look back on that as the one opportunity I'll have in my life to make a European Cup Final.

"I had a chance in the first half that was actually closer in than the one I scored but I chose to lay it back to Coisty when I should have had a crack.

"I've thought about that a couple of times and there was another break in the second half when I tried to play Ally in and Gary McSwegan was clean through.

"I didn't spot the runner and things like that prey on the mind even now."

Stroll past a Rangers training session at Glasgow's West of Scotland cricket ground these days and you might just hear a reminder of that night when the club came so close to the Final.

Wise-cracking Durrant has never let close pal McCoist forget about his Champions League exploits.

And he smiled: "I scored two goals on that run that will take a bit of beating – one against Bruges at Ibrox and THAT half-volley in Marseille.

"You know, every time a ball comes to me at training like that I scream 'Marseille!' at the top of my voice. The only problem is that these days it wallops some poor bugger on the back of the head and knocks them out.

"Seriously, it could have been

Rangers-AC Milan in the Final and people would have expected us to get hammered.

"I know that they were without question Europe's best but Marseille still beat them. We were on fire that season and who knows what would have happened?"

There's no question the failures in Europe have hurt everyone at Ibrox over the years but this was the one season when it all clicked.

It all began on September 16, 1992 at Ibrox when goals from Mark Hateley and Pieter Huistra got Gers through 2-0 on a nervy night against Danish champs Lyngby.

THE return in Copenhagen saw an incredible travelling army of 5,000 Light Blue foot soldiers. Durrant surged clear on a thrilling break to round the keeper and roll home the game's only goal and he recalled: "The tie gave us a great start and I can still remember the goal because the keeper went down early and made it very easy for me.

"That venue, the Parken Stadium, won't be remembered by many but it's the favourite one I've EVER played in.

"It was superb and we had a huge travelling support that night – it was a lovely feeling to score for them."

The feelgood factor stayed around for the second instalment of the competition as Rangers got the draw everyone wanted – The Battle of Britain. English champions Leeds United's route to the most talked about dust-up for years had been circuitous.

They looked destined for an exit against VFB Stuttgart but the Germans unwittingly played a fourth foreigner and a replay was ordered in Barcelona.

Howard Wilkinson's side won it 2-1 and the stage was set for a classic.

The atmosphere in the first leg at Ibrox on October 21 made the hairs on the backs of necks bristle. The noise was deafening.

Then Gary McAllister fizzed a brilliant volley into Andy Goram's top right hand corner and you could have heard a pin drop.

Gers needed a way back in and they found it through a calamitous error that forced every English jibe about dodgy Scottish keepers back down their throats.

Durrant swung in a corner and as John Lukic charged out he somehow managed to flail at the ball and send it behind him into his own net.

The midfielder grinned: "I couldn't believe it when Lukic claimed an own goal for punching in my corner.

"He said he lost it in the floodlights but it was clearly an old Durrant ploy, that extra bit of bend.

"Still I've had to get used to people

stealing goals off me – Laudrup did it with the strike at Celtic that all but clinched nine in a row."

As the stadium pulsed to a Rangers' beat after the equaliser, Dave McPherson powered in a header that was parried and McCoist swooped to bag the rebound.

Rangers were 2-1 up with the trip to England to come but they were still written off by almost every pundit down south.

Proving them wrong at Elland Road was to be the sweetest feeling and Ibrox diehard Ian – signed from kids side Glasgow United way back in 1984 – admitted: "The beating we gave Leeds is up there with the best memories I'll have when I finish playing."

IT was a season that brought the very best out of so many from the remarkable Andy Goram, through the grit of John Brown in defence to the tigerish Stuart McCall in midfield and the striking prowess of 49-goal Ally McCoist.

And if November 4 is to be remembered for one thing it must be Goram's defiance. He was almost superhuman that night, producing a string of saves that sickened the English.

And any time he was beaten a Gers body would pop up to clear the danger after Hateley set the tone with a thunderous second minute volley that dipped viciously over Lukic for the critical away goal.

Gers fanatic Brown couldn't have been more fired up – Leeds even chose the music to get him in the mood.

He revealed: "They had the theme from Rocky, Eye of the Tiger, pumping out when we walked down the tunnel and I think they thought that would intimidate us.

"But I turned round and there was wee Durrant shadow-boxing!

"We were ready for them and Andy had a night he should never forget."

After the break Durrant linked slickly with Hateley before the big striker produced the cross of his life for McCoist at the back post.

Ally's back-post diving header back against the balance of the keeper was perfect and it was all over despite a late Eric Cantona consolation goal. It was a sign of Rangers' resilience that season that they returned from Leeds – and the ensuing celebration party – to beat Celtic 1-0 away three days later.

Durrant once more was the man who mattered, this time latching on to a McCoist knockdown to score from close range.

And he's desperate to blow away what he considers a myth about that goal. He said: "McCoist has always claimed that setting me up for that goal was one of the great acts of footballing unselfishness.

"But I can tell you that the way the cross came to him (a) he doesn't have the technique to bring it down and score with two touches and (b) I've always felt he went to score with the header and it came off the wrong corner of his napper!"

Away from Scotland's pressures, though, Rangers were in with the elite now but they made the worst possible Champions League start against Marseille at Ibrox.

Alen Boksic ghosted into space to volley in the opener before German veteran Rudi Voller profited from a dreadful mix-up between Steven Pressley and Goram to make it two.

What followed was the essence of Rangers, the refusal to bow to defeat.

Sub Gary McSwegan rose to send a header swirling beyond Fabien Barthez from Alexei Mikhailitchenko's cross and suddenly French confidence was draining in the rain.

Then the tireless Durrant roared into the box and his cross flew into the path of Hateley who gleefully buried a diving header.

It was a point snatched from the snapping jaws of defeat and Ian reflected: "They let us out of jail after murdering us for most of the match.

"Yet if that game had gone another

'Fluke of his life but Nissy lapped up headlines'

five minutes we'd have WON."

Next on the agenda were Russian champs CSKA Moscow, forced into a neutral venue in Bochum in Germany because of the chilling severity of winter in their homeland.

That suited Smith's side and even without crocked Richard Gough they secured a 1-0 win thanks to Ian Ferguson's wickedly deflected drive to keep the pot boiling.

Bruges in Belgium on March 3, 1993 was a treacherous assignment in the first place. They hadn't been beaten at home in Europe for five years.

It became even tougher without the services of Gough, Gary Stevens, Trevor Steven, Ian Ferguson and Dale Gordon but Rangers rose to it.

Pieter Huistra capped a spirited comeback from one down when he latched on to a Stuart McCall miscue unselfishly left by McCoist to smash high into the net.

The return in Glasgow two weeks later was further evidence for a case

that should not be disputed, this was one of the truly great Rangers teams.

They were flowing sweetly and Durrant was on target once more, a goal he still cherishes after revealing: "Trevor Steven played me in with one of the best balls I've ever ran on to, inch-perfect and skidding along the surface despite the mud and glaur."

In the aftermath of the goal, though, Hateley became embroiled in a feud and was red-carded.

A BRUGES equaliser came quickly after the break through Lorenzo Stalens but Gers enjoyed a huge slice of luck with the winner – and you could have searched all of Scotland and never found a more delighted scorer.

Scott Nisbet, whose career was to be so cruelly cut short that season, saw his cross spin off a defender and spiral

into the air before skidding off the turf and arching over the head of bewildered keeper Danny Verlinden.

Durrant still smiles when he thinks back to Nissy's face as he was restrained by a UEFA official on the touchline while trying to reach the bench to celebrate.

And he said: "Once again I scored a cracker and big Nisbet flukes one and gets all the headlines, unbelievable.

"But people should look past how Scott scored and look at the achievement that night. We played with 10 men for 52 minutes yet we still won it."

Five years after the horrific knee injury that almost ended his playing days Durrant was back to his best throughout that campaign.

And he stressed: "That night against Bruges just summed up that season, yet it wasn't the first time I'd felt we were on the verge of a European trophy.

"Back in 1988 I felt we could have won it but we lost in the quarter-final

'To miss out on the Final was so painful'

to Steaua Bucharest. We let ourselves down in Romania and lost 2-0 then conceded a goal in the first minute at Ibrox and pummelled them only to win 2-1 and go out.

"We were well set that season because we'd signed Ian Ferguson, Mark Walters and John Brown and if we could have got past Steaua then they'd have been eligible for the semis.

"It has had its disappointments but I've always loved playing in Europe, I used to go and see the opposition teamsheets and see we were playing against names like Voller, Deschamps, Abedi Pele and van der Elst.

"If you don't get a buzz out of playing in that company then you'd be as well chucking it."

Durrant's current Ibrox deal runs out in 1998 and he knows time could be running out for him at the only club he's ever wanted to play for.

His heart was never really in a brief loan spell at Everton and he confessed: "I didn't enjoy it too much at Goodison and it will break my heart the day I walk out of Ibrox exit door.

"But everyone knows that with me it will never be for good.

"I'll be back as a fan and I have a shock for the punters because my masterplan is to one day come back as BOSS with McCoist as my No.2 and Ted McMinn running the reserves!"

THAT famous win over Bruges took Gers to Marseille for the match that became a tale of so near and yet so far but for John Brown it will always be the season of his life.

Like Durrant, Bomber had suffered the pain and frustration of injury when he was snubbed by Hearts on

the grounds of his fitness before Graeme Souness swooped. Now a key man on the backroom staff he would have been the fourth member of the nine-in-a-row club alongside Gough, McCoist and Ferguson if injury hadn't wrecked his 1996-97 hopes.

But as we sat in the marble hall at Ibrox the piercing eyes crinkled with humour when he remembered those days of glory in Europe.

And he said: "There were so many stories that make me laugh to this day.

"My mate from the Thornliebank supporters' bus had been away for three days in Bruges and jumped off the bus with the cry 'I want to get some good Scottish grub down my neck' – so he leapt off and went for a Chinky!

"Then there was one of the players' mothers who on the way back from Marseille explained to someone why the return journey would take 45 minutes longer.

"I'm not lying when I tell you she said 'The reason is that it's night time this time and the pilot can't see where he's going."

Wearing your heart on your sleeve in football has become unfashionable these days, it's far trendier to have your agent make sure your hefty wallet is tucked away in the inside pocket of your Versace jacket.

BUT Brown won't change, he remains a fan who made it to play for the club he loves and he said: "We were so close then. Yet we can take so much pride out of that run because looking over the two games against Marseille, McCoist missed the first because he was injured and Hateley was banned for the second.

"I often wonder what would have happened if we could have had the two of them together for those matches.

"To be undefeated in Europe over a season and not make the Final was so bitterly disappointing."

He's right. To put the achievement into context, Alex Ferguson's Manchester United lost five times in Europe in '96-97 and were lauded for reaching the last four.

It all ended on April 21 with an agonising night against CSKA Moscow when every aerial chance that Hateley would have gobbled up fell to McCoist.

Ally couldn't buy a break and as Marseille won in Bruges Rangers drew 0-0, the final curtain came down on a dramatic story.

Rangers were out and the players slumped to the turf in dejection, Gough with a seeping head wound, Goram with his shirt soaked in sweat, McCoist overcome by emotion.

They had given it all. The blood, the sweat and the tears.

SIX IN A ROW

Scottish Premier

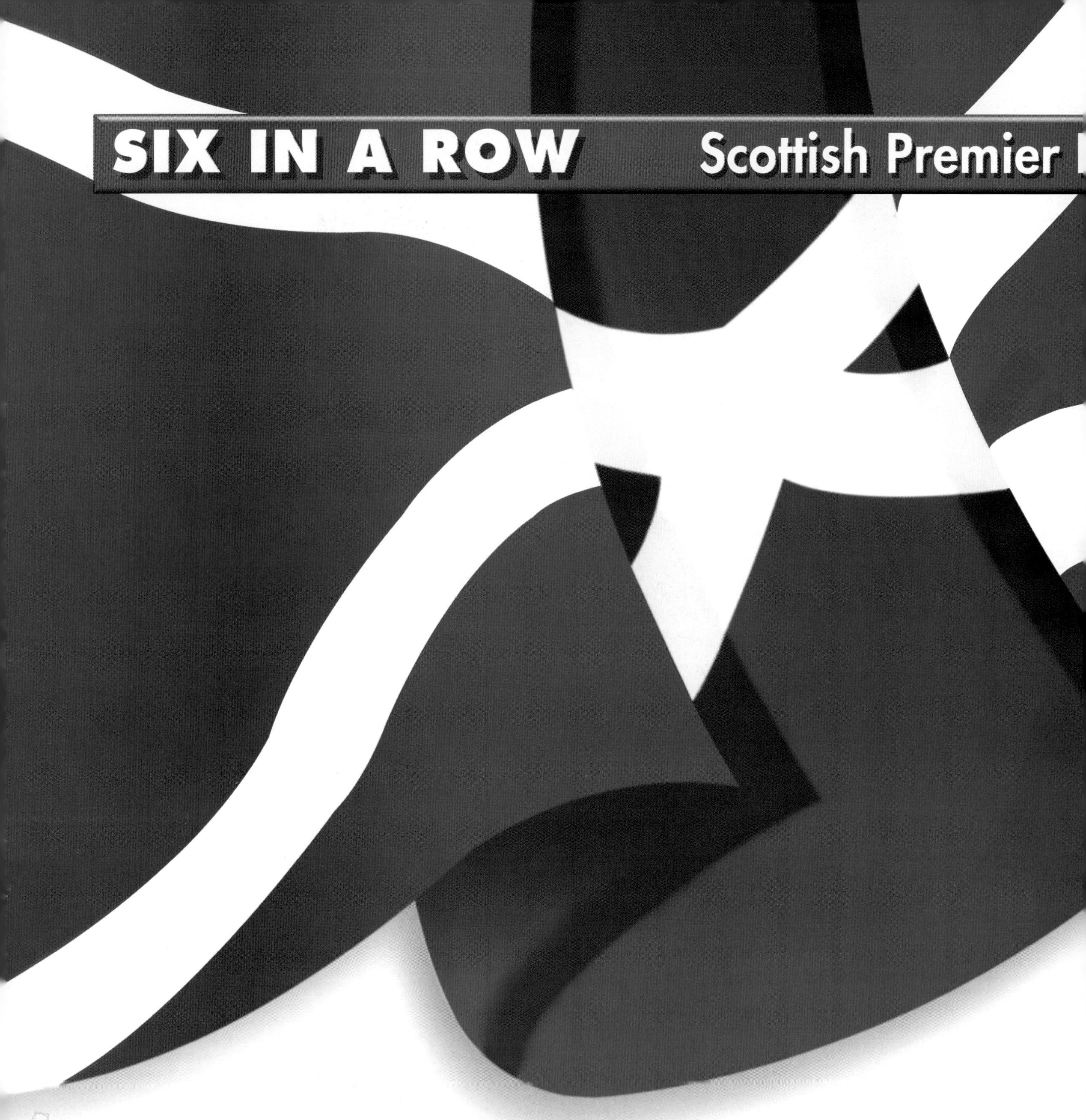

This chapter is brought to you
in association with

AON

Aon Risk Services

CHAPTER 6

BACK-TO-BACK trebles – it was a dream nurtured at the start of the season and fuelled by the £4.1 million arrival of Duncan Ferguson from Dundee United.

Despite a crippling catalogue of injuries, Rangers – dogged and spirited this time rather than daring and sparkling – almost made it happen.

Sadly, the dream died in the Ibrox treatment room rather than on the pitch, as the gruelling schedule of the previous two years finally caught up with crucial players like Ally McCoist and Andy Goram.

Typically, McCoist still conjured up one magical moment to win the League Cup against Hibs after an early European Cup exit at the hands of Bulgarians Levski Sofia left the club demoralised. And with Player of the Year Mark Hateley outstanding and midfielders Stuart McCall and Ian Ferguson inspirational, Rangers wrapped up the title.

The season, though, was to end in bitter disappointment as the team – by now jaded and fading – lost the Scottish Cup Final to Dundee United to scorn a chance of history.

SCORE POINT...
Stuart McCall celebrates a goal, but like so many other Rangers stars, injury was to take its toll during 1993/94

Rangers showing signs of flagging

THE crate of beer lay on the dressing-room floor untouched. A championship had been won but Rangers' title heroes left Easter Road defeated and dejected.

It was the picture that told the story of a season – the tale of a campaign that started with hopes soaring and ended with two glittering trophies. Yet it will always be haunted by a feeling of what might have been.

Rangers were to finish an injury-marred campaign dog-tired and in tears after a shock Scottish Cup final defeat by Ivan Golac's Dundee United ruined the dream of successive trebles.

Still, a League Cup and title double should have been seen as a triumph of spirit for a squad stricken by the loss of key players all season.

But midfield dynamo Stuart McCall gave a telling insight into the Ibrox mentality as he looked back at this, the year when nine-in-a-row could have been smashed to bits.

He said: "For me, we won two honours that season but we were average.

"We'd set high standards the season before that and we didn't match them. I regard that season as a failure.

"Looking back over history, people will point to the treble teams of 1976 and 1978, but I think of the previous season's as the most successful Rangers side ever.

"Not only had we won the treble, we'd gone 44 games unbeaten and ten games in Europe without defeat.

"And, remember, if we'd beaten Marseille away, we'd have made the European Cup Final.

"In 1992-93, players like Andy Goram, John Brown, Richard Gough, Ian Durrant,

HEIGHT OF AGONY...
Duncan Ferguson
never got the chance
to live
up to his £4.1
million billing

'Rangers risked a bundle on 6ft 3ins of raw potential'

Ally McCoist and myself had the season of our lives.

"We looked forward to the next season so much but deep down the strain on our bodies was starting to tell.

"As it turned out, if anyone was going to take the league away from us, this was the year to do it."

Walter Smith's treble heroes were to be joined by just one big-name signing that summer as the entire transfer budget – all £4.1million of it – was used to prise Duncan Ferguson from Dundee United.

Rangers had risked a bundle on 6ft 3ins of raw, rugged striking potential, just 21 years old.

The fans were never to see the investment pay off.

Big Dunc – plagued by off-the-field troubles and court cases after becoming involved in stupid clashes with the law as a United player – toiled with injury as Mark Hateley prospered.

The Englishman was a decade older than the kid threatening his jersey, but he also had ten years more experience to draw on. He used every shred of it that season and by the end of it all, the fortunes of the two

strikers couldn't have been more contrasting. Hateley was deservedly the Player of the Year and still at the peak of his profession.

Ferguson had started just seven league games and was embroiled in controversy over a headbutt on Raith Rovers' John McStay that was to cost him 44 days in Barlinnie Prison after he'd moved to Everton.

As Ferguson checked in during the summer, Dale Gordon was checking out for West Ham in an £800,000 switch.

He was soon followed by reserve striker Gary McSwegan, who went to Notts County in a £400,000 deal, carrying with him the precious memory of a stunning header against Marseille the previous season.

The squad that started

the season against Hearts on August 7 was saddened by the news that pelvic trouble had forced Scott Nisbet (below left) to quit the game at the age of just 25 – injury was to become the recurring theme.

Stuart recalled: "I came off in the first league game with a hernia problem that had been caused by all the games we had played in the marvellous season before. We were to miss Andy Goram and Ally McCoist for large chunks of that season, Dave McPherson had an operation and John Brown went under the knife too.

"I've always looked back upon that as the Year of the Hernia! Seriously, the season before, we'd been playing big games every week and if your groin gets a little tear, you can leave it a week, rest and still play.

"No-one wanted to miss games, so that's what they'd do. But it was to catch up with us all eventually.

"Hardly anyone trained that season – it became a strict workout regime of baths and bacon rolls!"

Young striker David Hagen made the most of a rare start to fire the champs in front on opening day.

The second was vintage Hateley, as he met Ian Durrant's corner with a thumping header to seal a 2-1 win.

Sick Stuart could only watch from the bench as Attila went on the rampage once more, but he sensed an inner fire burning inside his fiercely competitive soul.

He insisted: "When big Dunc arrived, it was both a threat and a spur for Hateley.

"I was sharing a room with Mark at our training camp at I1 Ciocco in Tuscany when Duncan was signed and he was stunned.

"He knew the manager didn't want Ferguson as a left winger. They were the same type of player and they would be playing for the same position."

That joust for the jersey

*THAT'S MY SEAT…
Hateley made sure
Duncan Ferguson got
to know the Ibrox
pecking order*

'Hateley saw big Dunc as a rival'

up front was to lead to one of the most famous Glasgow pub stories of all time.

Legend had it that Ferguson's sense of dressing-room fun had led him to redesign some of Hateley's designer gear – and earned him a punch in the face.

But Stuart smiled: "I can exclusively reveal that Duncan Ferguson didn't cut the lapels off Mark's Versace jacket!

"It's true Hateley saw big Dunc as a rival, though, and one revealing little incident does tell you something.

"We're all numbered in the dressing-room with a number you're given when you join the club.

"For instance, I'm No.3, because that's what was available when I joined the club.

"Big Mark was 14 and Ally, of course, was 9. On big Dunc's first day, I remember that 10 had become available and Ferguson walked in and changed there beside McCoist.

"Mark was peeved by this, obviously thinking 'He's getting a rapport going and changing next to my striking partner'.

"The next morning, all the kit had been changed and Hateley was 10 and Dunc was bombed down to 14.

"When he was asked why, Mark growled 'Ten is my number off AND on the park'."

Hateley was to be on the mark once more in a very special match for a striker who will deservedly stroll into the Ibrox Hall of Fame when he tearfully hangs up his scoring boots.

Ally McCoist MBE has for years been Rangers' most explosive scorer, the striker

Walter Smith once tagged a "lucky so and so."

Apparently, McCoist once fell into the Clyde and came out wearing a diver's watch with a salmon in his pocket.

So it was a rare stroke of ill fortune that saw him still sidelined by the broken leg he'd suffered playing for Scotland and sitting out his own testimonial match.

But the punters he'd long-since won over after a rocky start way back in 1983 weren't about to let him forget just what he meant to them.

Over 42,000 turned up on an emotional night against the emerging Newcastle United.

Goals from Andy Cole and Scott Sellers dumped Rangers, yet this was one night when defeat didn't taste too sour.

INSTEAD, it was a night to honour a player whose contribution to the Light Blue cause won't be fully appreciated until the day he's no longer around to flash that famous goalscorer's smile.

Back on league business, Rangers travelled to St Johnstone to clock up a 2-1 win, sealed by a goal from a midfield mainstay in a Light Blues jersey.

Ian Ferguson played 35 league games that season – only Hateley and skipper Richard Gough played more – and for once he steered clear of injury and illness.

He confessed: "That has been a rare feeling for me and I've had some dark days and so much frustration.

"But if I asked you the names of the three players who have all nine medals from the nine-in-a-row run, you'd be hard pushed to get

the answer. It's Richard Gough, Ally McCoist and Ian Ferguson and I'm proud of that."

As injuries bit deep into Rangers' resources that season, Fergie was to be a key figure and the scale of the crisis was never more emphatically illustrated than in the first Old Firm game of the season.

Manager Smith went in with seven international players sidelined and with keeper Ally Maxwell and defenders Fraser Wishart – a free transfer from Falkirk – and Steven Pressley facing Celtic for the first time.

Duncan Ferguson almost grabbed a glory winner with two flashes of brilliance, but the 0-0 draw was a credit to a makeshift side.

The bubble, though, was about to burst.

Ibrox on August 28 signalled what was to be the start of a worrying trait that had never troubled the champs before – home defeats.

Kilmarnock battered their way into a shock lead with a diving header from 17-year-old striker Mark Roberts. Although Pressley equalised, Rangers were destined to end up with nothing.

Maxwell fumbled a shot and former Ibrox striker Bobby Williamson twisted the knife with the injury-time winner.

The Rangers keeper would face many more tests of his character and many more searching questions before he could emerge from this troubled season with a championship medal.

Rangers shook off the shock of that Killie KO to win an epic League Cup quarter-final with Aberdeen thanks to an extra-time clincher from Ian Ferguson, but their title hopes were

'I ended up feeling sorry for Duncan'

SLIM CHANCE… a rare strike from Dave McPherson helped Rangers to a 3-2 European win at home to Levski Sofia

plummeting. Goals from Hateley were the only moments to savour in abject 1-1 draws with Dundee and Partick Thistle. Against Jags, big Dunc hared away on one of the most memorable Ibrox celebrations, only to see his "goal" disallowed.

That game was to be one of the few times the two dominating front men played together – the mix wasn't right and their teammates knew it.

McCall said: "The boss tried them in the same team but it was never going to work.

"They were both big guys and they both naturally drifted left onto their strong foot.

"But that little bit of a threat inspired Hateley to great things and I ended up feeling sorry for Duncan.

"Rangers would have liked to take him a season later but that was when the deal came up and they went for it.

"Leeds United had offered a lot of money and if he'd gone there he might have been lost to Ibrox, so they moved quickly.

"But Mark played out of his skin and Ferguson never really got a chance."

It was against this unsettled striking backdrop that the early test of Rangers' readiness for battle against the elite of Europe came, in the shape of unfancied Bulgarians, Levski Sofia.

Rangers were to turn in a performance that summed up their disjointed start and they gifted two sloppy away goals in a 3-2 win that featured another Hateley double and a rare strike from the underrated McPherson.

A 2-0 defeat at Aberdeen had the chins on the floor once more, but this was to be a season of resolve and Rangers, wounded and stricken by that casualty list, were ready to show their claws.

The League Cup semi-final with Celtic at Ibrox seemed certain to be another mission in misery when Peter Huistra was red-carded for a stupid kick at Tom Boyd.

Once more, just as they had in the Scottish Cup semi-final in 1992, Rangers had to face the Hoops with ten men. Once more, they were to beat them.

This time, a fatal error in judgement from Celt Mike Galloway allowed the ever-alert Ian Durrant in to speed clear. The cross was perfect and Hateley scored from

'Hateley inspired all of us'

WATCH AND LEARN...
Ian Ferguson says Rangers owe a debt to Hateley's 93-94 exploits

close range to send the home fans into delirium.

For Ian Ferguson, big Mark's clincher summed up what he believes was the hit-man's best season in Rangers colours.

Fergie revealed: "Hateley inspired all of us. He wasn't just setting goals up as we'd come to expect from him, but he was scoring them too.

"He won Player of the Year and never has it been more deserved. There were times when he was carrying us through just with his strength and his sheer will to win."

A 2-1 win over Hibs sent the players into Bulgaria with their confidence flooding back but rollercoaster Rangers suffered the European Cup second leg of their nightmares.

Durrant's goal had Smith's side easing towards the Champions League but, with the game tied at 1-1, they were sent careering out of Europe in heartbreaking fashion as the seconds ticked away.

McCall, rushed back from his hernia operation to skipper the side in that first leg, groaned: "I was closing Nikolai Todorov

down and I was actually thinking to myself 'hit it'.

"He'd been firing them high and wide all night but he caught it superbly and it flew into the postage stamp corner. We were out.

"We hadn't had a spectacular start to the season and we were drawing way too many games.

"The flak was flying and confidence wasn't too high. Now this.

"It was an awful blow and everyone tried to pick themselves up with the notion of doing a double treble.

"But, to be honest, the hangover from that game stayed with us."

Rangers were still suffering when they travelled to Kirkcaldy for a 1-1 draw with Raith and a dismal 2-1 home defeat by Motherwell once more had the prophets of doom predicting the end of the club's title sequence.

Yet there were signs that Rangers could get out of the rut at Tannadice on October 9, when Dutch winger Huistra rifled home two stunning goals and Hateley grabbed another in a thrilling 3-1 win.

The maelstrom of Scottish football sometimes

MR MOTIVATOR… as Celtic's Peter Grant knows only too well, Player of the Year Mark Hateley was a force to be reckoned with in a testing season for Rangers

'They savour trophies all the more'

SILVERSMITH...
Walter adds
another trophy
to the Ibrox
collection

threatened to engulf Blue Pieter in his early days at the club but by 1993 he'd found a little more dig to spice up his deft play.

Stuart pointed out: "Huistra had this daunting task in front of him, playing in a jersey that had previously been filled by Davie Cooper and Mark Walters.

"Although he was a different sort of player, he did a great job.

"Pieter and David Robertson had an excellent partnership and Davie loved to play with him because he was clever enough to work back when Robbo went forward.

"They were good friends off the pitch and constantly talked about how to improve the link-up."

SING WHEN YOU'RE WINNING… and a familiar end-of-season celebration for the Rangers stars

The H-Bomb partnership of Huistra and Hateley came up trumps again in a 2-0 Ibrox win over St Johnstone before McCoist, the author of football fairytales, penned another unlikely chapter in his career.

October 24 at Parkhead brought a League Cup final against Hibs and a conclusion which Rangers diehards, who'd suffered the mediocrity before the Souness Revolution, must have prayed for.

Durrant and McCoist will always have a special bond with a support who regard them as their own kind.

In the days of £15,000-a-week glamour foreign imports, these wisecracking fans-turned-players are the double act from the dark days.

Before the glory times, Ian and Ally toiled away alongside players who didn't deserve to wear the famous Light Blue jersey.

THEIR bitter experience as Ibrox also-rans means they now savour the trophies all the more and against Hibees they plundered the goals in a memorable 2-1 win.

Durrant expertly lifted the first over Jim Leighton before comeback king McCoist – nowhere near full fitness but an inspirational choice on the bench – made a never-to-be-forgotten entry into the fray after McPherson's own-goal had levelled the match.

A long throw-in looked to be bobbing aimlessly in the box until the supersub launched into an incredible overhead kick to send the ball arrowing into the far corner.

To this day, McCall laughs his socks off when he recalls that goal.

He smiled: "He was so fat and unfit that when he landed, there was a roundabout left in the penalty box where he fell!

"It was a no-go area for the rest of the match. People had to run round it in case they fell in.

"But anyone who knows Ally knows that he really is Roy of the Rovers. I knew he would score, but what I didn't know was that it would be an overhead kick."

The first trophy of the season was resting at Ibrox but, six days later, two Hallowe'en howlers from Maxwell had all the old worries haunting the place again.

There is no more unforgiving arena for a Rangers keeper to make errors than an Old Firm game, and Ally would never really be allowed to forget the gaffes that handed goals to John Collins and Brian O'Neil to give Celtic a 2-1 win.

McCall felt nothing but sympathy for the former Motherwell No.1. He said: "Ally Maxwell had the hardest job in football, taking over from Andy Goram.

"We were losing more games than the fans were used to and he became the scapegoat for that.

129

'Spitting was the wrong way to react'

OFF NIGHT.. Ian Ferguson is given his marching orders after a spitting incident with Gordan Petric. Ironically the big Serb, pictured right in that season's cup final, was later to become Fergie's team-mate

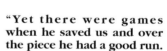

"Yet there were games when he saved us and over the piece he had a good run.

"There will come a time again when Andy Goram isn't No.1 at Rangers and I would never envy the next man to have that jersey."

Rangers steadied the ship in November with a 2-2 draw at Hearts before key midfielder Ferguson hit the scoresheet again in wins over Kilmarnock and Dundee as McCoist hirpled onto the sidelines for three more months.

Another damaging draw was just around the corner as Rangers were held 2-2 at home by Raith and a narrow 1-0 squeak over Hibs – a game that signalled the arrival of Gordon Durie from Tottenham Hotspur – was followed by yet another slip with a point dropped at Partick Thistle.

There is no doubt reflecting on the history that has been made in 1997 that a footballing milestone could have been reduced to rubble in this campaign.

But Aberdeen, Motherwell and fourth-placed Celtic weren't up to the task and with the star names missing so often the engine room of McCall, Ferguson and the cultured Trevor Steven became ever more

vital. A 2-0 win over the Dons paved the way for a day Durie had dreamed of since he imitated his Rangers heroes in the park as a kid.

He'd gone a long way round through East Fife, Hibs, Chelsea and Spurs to get to Ibrox but with £4.1m Dunc injured his signing was to prove a Smith masterstroke as Jukebox rattled in 12 league goals to help his stuttering club over the finishing line.

Durie broke his duck with a sparkling double at 'Well in a 2-0 win but a week later midweek sidekick Ferguson's season threat-ened to collapse in disarray after a spitting storm that still shames him four years on.

Rangers went into a December 11 home clash with Dundee United looking more assured but it was a facade, they were behind to a Dave Bowman goal within 21 SECONDS and Paddy Connolly and Craig Brewster had them 3-0 down inside 21 minutes!

As Smith's side fell to pieces an infuriated Ferguson reacted to a challenge from Gordan Petric – ironically later to be his teammate – by spitting on the United player.

Crestfallen and embarrassed, he apologised immediately after the match but he was hit with a six-match ban and he recalled: "It was the worst possible thing I could have done, I still cringe when I think about it.

"I've spoken to Gordan since and he knows he was elbowing all day, he could have broken my jaw or my nose and I was furious when he tried the same with Gordon Durie and Mark Hateley.

"But that was never the way to react and I sure as Hell knew that by the media reaction afterwards.

"I was hounded for two weeks and I felt like a murderer – yet it was a lesson to me that everything you do as a Rangers player has consequences.

"I was ashamed of myself that day and when I think back I still am, I let down myself, my family and the club.

"The day Gordan walked into Ibrox a Rangers player I walked over first and shook his hand to welcome him.

"I'll always be embarrassed by that day, you'll always win more respect by thumping into a honest tackle than resorting to spitting."

We had to start well and within a minute we were 1-0 up

Suddenly, all Ferguson's hard work meant nothing as he was booted onto the sidelines but it was to be a season when a patched-up team responded to adversity.

Hateley grabbed back-to-back doubles in a 4-0 win at St Johnstone and a 2-2 home draw with Hearts before a Ne'erday clash with Celtic that at last ignited a run to the title.

It was the day when the Russian connection finally clicked and McCall looked back and said: "Going into the game at Celtic we were underdogs for the first time in a long while.

"That was the turning point and I remember reading Billy McNeill's newspaper column all about how Celtic were going to win.

"The Gaffer stressed to us that we had to start well and within a minute we were ahead."

Hateley, so often the hammer of the Celts, claimed that dramatic opener and by the 29th minute it was 3-0 thanks to a double from Alexei Mikhailitchenko. Oleg Kuznetsov then bombed in a classic second-half volley as Rangers eased to a 4-2 win

that was the catalyst in a 17-game unbeaten run – the charge to the championship.

Killie were hammered 3-0 before draws with Dundee and challengers Aberdeen simply lit the blue touch paper for the long-awaited fireworks of a perplexing campaign.

February flew in as McCall hit the target in a 5-1 romp against Partick Thistle before Ferguson returned to salvage his season in the 2-0 win over Hibs that saw McCoist and Goram's long-awaited first team returns.

Fergie then also claimed a crucial strike in a 2-1 win at Raith.

March 5 saw title-chasing Motherwell stride into Ibrox and silence the home fans with a goal of stunning quality from Paul Lambert who crashed home a

thrilling 30-yarder as Rangers retreated.

Almost at once Rangers were level when Durie smashed a shot straight at the grounded Rab McKinnon and the ball veered into the net.

It was the slice of luck the champions needed and John Philliben's ill-advised handball gave Hateley the ultimate test of nerve from the spot in the dying seconds.

The big man was up to the task and the 2-1 win put his side on the home straight.

Triumphs over St Johnstone, Hearts and Partick then racked up a sequence of seven straight wins that must have kicked the heart out of a chasing pack who this time really did have Rangers' scent in their nostrils. Draws with the Dons

and Dundee United were good enough to keep the Ibrox men on course and at Tannadice Hateley was rested to allow fit-again Duncan Ferguson back into the limelight briefly.

A poor display in a 0-0 Scottish Cup semi-final draw with Kilmarnock meant a replay the club didn't need but Hateley dredged up a hotly-disputed equaliser before Durie left tackles in his wake to set Mark up for the winner.

On April 16 against Raith big Dunc was again the focus of attention and he was never to be out of the headlines for all the wrong reasons.

Ferguson and the club he loved should have been a perfect footballing marriage, instead it finished up in the courts and he ended up in prison.

Those prior convictions he'd amassed in his days on Tayside were to weigh heavily on the troubled striker when, despite the fact that he received just a booking from ref Kenny Clark, he was later found guilty of headbutting Raith's John McStay.

In a cruel twist it all happened during a 4-0 win when he scored the first league goal he'd waited eight months for.

The storm threatened to overshadow the team's critical run-in to six-in-a-row but Durie did his duty once more with a double in a 2-1 success over Dundee United in what was to be a Cup Final rehearsal.

But just when it seemed the team were marching towards another Treble things started to go wrong.

Stuart sighed: "We were on a great run and then we lost 2-1 away to lose our unbeaten run at Motherwell and it began to turn sour."

Defeat at Fir Park came at further cost with keeper Maxwell injured, now Rangers were down to third choice Colin Scott with the final four games of the season looming.

First up was Celtic and Smith's side knew victory could clinch the title in front of a partisan crowd, every one of them a Rangers supporter. Ibrox chairman David Murray had taken the decision to ban the Hoops' fans after vandalism at a previous Ibrox showdown but the absence of their vocal backing seemed to inspire Lou Macari's side.

John Collins swerved one of his trademark free-kicks beyond Scott and although Mikhailitchenko conjured up a solo run and a deflected finish the champagne was on ice.

What followed in mid-week at Hibs was one of the biggest anti-climaxes of this famous nine-in-a-row run as Keith Wright's goal condemned Gers to defeat.

Elsewhere, Motherwell had lost at home to Dundee United and the title was forlornly wrapped up in red, white and blue ribbons.

For McCall, who'd come back off the operating table

to be a driving force, and Ferguson – who'd grimly battled through his fall from grace – it was a sickener.

And Stuart recalled: "I remember the Gaffer coming in so frustrated and annoyed with our display and I sat there thinking: "What a disappointment."

"Some of the punters didn't even know we'd won it and we rightly got some boos on the way off because we'd been terrible.

"For a team that could have won the title in style we'd blown it.

"Someone arranged for a crate of beer to be brought into the dressing-room and it lay there untouched."

The journey to Glasgow as champions was quiet and subdued and it was 50 miles

that Fergie will never forget.

He groaned: "It was awful, you look forward to that feeling of being a winner – it's what a season's work is all about.

"Yet this just didn't feel right, it was weird. The usual card school between Hateley, McCoist and McCall was postponed and even John Brown and I sat quietly when we'd usually be chatting away.

"The atmosphere was falling flat and we weren't playing well, yet there was still a Treble to go for.

"The overpowering feeling that night wasn't that it had been a triumph, it had been a grind."

Now boss Smith was sweating, the players were either faded, jaded or fearing

'I know we missed out on history'

suspension and it was a cobbled together side that then lost 1-0 at Killie.

But even with many of the big guns back in the final home league game with Dundee the best Rangers could manage was a 0-0 draw.

The Cup Final with Dundee United was now upon a side who hadn't won in five games and McCall revealed: "I watched the manager in the build-up to the Final and he was a worried man – he was 100 per cent right to feel like that.

"We hadn't won any of the last five games and we were toiling to score, the sharpness and the edge had gone.

"I remember us being odds-on but it all went so flat despite the boss and Archie trying to gee everyone up."

History beckoned Rangers on May 21, 1994 but the goal they lost to United summed up a season that had touched the heights and plumbed the depths.

McPherson was a little short with a passback and Maxwell hammered his clearance against Christian Dailly whose shot rolled across the Hampden turf and off the post for Brewster to gleefully smack home.

Rangers had nothing left to give and Stuart admitted:

"There was one word to describe the closing stages that season – FLAT.

"We'd lost away at Well, drawn at home to Celtic when we could have clinched it, won the title when we got beat and then drew the last game 0-0 when we got the trophy.

"That Final was the most disappointing game of my LIFE, we lost a dreadful goal and it was an enormous downer.

"I look back now years on and know we missed out on history without giving it our best shot and it still cuts me."

As we sat in the Ibrox Press Room to look back on this season, McCall shifted uncomfortably as the brace protecting his injured knee bothered him.

The cladding supporting his damaged ligaments was like a throwback, a reminder to that campaign when the stresses of life at the top of football caught up with so many at Ibrox.

And Stuart said: "That League Cup Final win, the 10-man win over Celtic and the New Year win over them were the highlights but it was a gruelling season.

"I remember being asked by the *Rangers News* to name my favourite six games and struggling to name three or four whereas the season before I could have named 26!"

FEW REALISE SUCH MAJOR ACHIEVEMENTS

'FIFTY IN A ROW'

50 YEARS

Riley Advertising Scotland

...ision Champions 1994-95

This chapter is brought to you
in association with

Galloway
Scottish Cheddar Cheese

CHAPTER 7

GENIUS is an over-used word in football, often bestowed on those who do not deserve it – this season saw the discovery of one who genuinely merited the mantle while another was tragically ripped away from us.

Brian Laudrup arrived from Fiorentina for £2.2million, in what must now be looked upon as a transfer heist by Walter Smith, and inspired his new club to the championship a massive 15 points clear of Motherwell.

Defeat in Europe by AEK Athens was hugely disappointing, a shock Coca-Cola Cup exit at the hands of Falkirk and a Scottish Cup reverse at Hearts hurt too.

But all that was put into sudden perspective behind a veil of tears as Rangers and Scottish football lost Davie Cooper.

At the tragically early age of 39, the former Ibrox idol was struck down by a brain haemorrhage while training children. Not only Rangers, but his other clubs, Clydebank and Motherwell, went into mourning.

They knew they would never see his like again.

A tale of two geniuses

GREAT Dane Brian Laudrup had become a football prisoner in Italy – then Walter Smith took the shackles off.

Laudrup was a shock summer signing from Fiorentina as Basile Boli checked in from Marseille to complete £5million worth of high-profile business.

Their impact on Scot-land's biggest club could not nave been more contrasting.

Laudrup rocked a host of top continental sides when he plumped for Rangers but Smith's sales pitch had worked perfectly – and when his reign ends as Rangers boss this capture will surely be looked upon as a landmark.

The cultured forward had the world at his feet after shining for Denmark – a last-minute replacement for war-torn Yugoslavia – as they marched to that remarkable European Championship triumph in 1992.

But it had all turned sour in Italy's Serie A as he struggled with relegation-haunted Fiorentina before a loan spell at AC Milan.

There he was to spend more time in the stands than on the pitch as multi-millionaire owner Silvio Berlusconi stockpiled a host of top-name foreigners.

So in 1994, at the age of 25, Brian Laudrup – who had already seen service with Brondby in Denmark and Bayer Uerdingen and Bayern Munich in Germany before his Italian adventure – stood at the crossroads of his career.

The route he chose shocked some experts and

WING WIZARDS...
Just as the Rangers fans were hailing Brian Laudrup as one of the best players to wear the light blue jersey, the tragic news broke of the death of the legendary Davie Cooper

*ON THE MOVE...
Laudrup was desperate
to escape the pressures
of Italian football – and
Walter Smith gave him
that opportunity*

'We were smuggled away in a car boot'

horrified many in a homeland where Brian and brother Michael are revered like royalty.

Yet it's a move he has never once regretted although he confessed: "I had several options at the time and I have to admit that at first I did not think Rangers was the place for me.

"The other offers came from Barcelona and other clubs in Spain and I was sick of that sort of scene where football is the absolute be all and end all.

"To me if there is one thing they will say about Brian Laudrup when he retires it should be that he

realised this is just a game, something to be played for fun. A chance to entertain people."

FROM his league debut against Motherwell when he veered cross-field on a searing 60-yard run beating tackle after tackle before setting up Duncan Ferguson's winner, Laudrup would do just that – entertain.

He had been given his freedom back by a manager who refused to place tactical constraints on him and he

flourished, picking up Player of the Year awards from both his fellow pros and the football writers.

It was a season in stark contrast to what he had gone through in Italy.

At Fiorentina the fervour of fans, stoked up by promises of the title, boiled over to make Laudrup's life a nightmare.

Brian and German midfielder Steffen Effenberg had been bought to bring glory to Florence, and when things went wrong they were cast as the scapegoats.

And he shuddered: "I remember standing at training one day and looking across to a fan with hate all

over his face who was ready to pitch an egg at me.

"I thought then that was not what football was supposed to be about.

"We were smuggled away from the training ground in car boots when it all started to slide and they pelted the team bus with stones after defeats, it became miserable."

Buying a footballing genius like Laudrup is one thing for a manager, resisting the temptation to tinker with his talent another.

Smith was to give a troubled player a place to play with a smile on his face again and Scotland gave Brian and wife Mette the place to raise

'Scotland became my escape from the pressure'

their family in peace – it was the perfect combination.

Laudrup had moved to the beautiful city of Florence with high hopes and he recalled : "I had been played just behind the main two strikers in all the pre-season friendlies but then when the season started the coach got cold feet and stuck me in a wide right defensive role.

"It worked for a while but then the wheels came off and I could not believe the reaction.

"I have never had any problems with people living on their fanatical passion inside a stadium.

"But when they carry it on outside then it starts to become an intrusion into the private family life that I value dearly.

"In Italy with Fiorentina everything was so black and white – when it blew up they were not trying to kiss me!"

T HE Milan sojourn left him feeling unwanted and unfulfilled and Smith swooped. Brian vowed to use his bitter experience to his advantage in his new environment and he stressed: "Critics said I had gone there too young but my brother Michael was

19 when he went to Italy and I think we both have the mentality to cope.

"I do not look upon it with happiness but it meant that when I eventually came to Rangers I was more experienced and I knew what I was looking for.

"Walter Smith sold Rangers to me and I knew straight away that I was dealing with a man of honesty and integrity.

"He told me he would take the shackles off and just let me play and he has been true to his word.

"It sounds strange when you play in a divided city, but Scotland became my escape from the pressure."

The heat was on Laudrup and his team-mates right away, though, as his first season began with a challenging away tie in Europe against AEK Athens on August 10, three days before the league campaign even started.

Rangers weren't anywhere near ready and amid the flares and fury of a sultry Greek night they were humbled 2-0.

The Premier bid then began against a Motherwell side who were to emerge as Rangers most serious challengers that season and it took the first real glimpse of Laudrup's gifts to sway it the way of the champions.

ELBOW GREECED...
The AEK Athens
tie came too
early for the new
boys at Ibrox

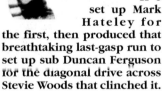

'Goram blasted his way back into the team'

He set up Mark Hateley for the first, then produced that breathtaking last-gasp run to set up sub Duncan Ferguson for the diagonal drive across Stevie Woods that clinched it.

A 2-0 win at Partick Thistle kept Rangers on track but within three gut-wrenching games boss Smith was to find himself staring at a season that was threatening to blow up in his face.

The return with AEK needed Gers to give the performance of their Euro lives and land a healthy slice of luck to help them through – Smith got neither.

Instead striker Toni Savevski's goal heaped insult onto injury and once more Scotland's much-vaunted champions were out at the first hurdle.

THREE days later Ibrox was plunged further into despair as Celtic stormed to a 2-0 Old Firm win thanks to goals from Paul McStay and John Collins and the fans felt things just couldn't get any worse. They were wrong.

The night of August 31 offered Rangers a chance of redemption with a Coca-Cola Cup clash at home to a Falkirk side that Jim Jefferies would take to the brink of European football.

It was a game that brought Laudrup's first goal for Rangers and precious little else for the Light Blues' Legions to cheer.

Richard Cadette fired the Bairns ahead only for Laudrup to smuggle an Ian Durrant cross away from Hateley and shoot the Ibrox men level.

Little Richie had the last word with the winner, though, and now the alarm bells were clanging at Ibrox.

Brian recalled: "Before I knew it I was in the middle of my first Ibrox crisis, three defeats in a week and they all came on our own turf.

"It was all happening so quickly then and I always feel it's very difficult for Rangers when we face that European preliminary round with a lot of new faces trying to gel together.

"I hadn't expected to hit top form until around October when I'd adjusted to my new surroundings but the fact was we were out of Europe already and it was bitterly disappointing".

Yet it was one incident in the wake of that Athens

IN FOR KEEPS....
*Walter Smith's shock
treatment helped
Andy Goram secure a
new deal at Rangers*

defeat that made Laudrup
determined to turn the season around.

He explained: "I remem-
ber after the AEK game I was
wary of walking through the
fans to get to my car after all
those bad experiences in
Florence.

"But as I came out there
was this cheer and people
were telling me to keep my
chin up that they knew I
was going to be a star for
Rangers – I knew then that
I'd made the right move.

"From that moment I
knew I could relax and play
my football at a special club.

"I still shudder to think
what the fans would have

done if we'd had a week like
that at Fiorentina."

For all the fighting talk
there was no hiding the fact
that Rangers were on the
rack but in a live Sunday
clash with Hearts in front of
Scotland's armchair mil-
lions Laudrup began to
weave his spells.

He twisted and turned,
teased and tormented the
Jambos defence into sub-
mission and set up two for
Hateley before strolling off
to a hero's ovation 13 minutes from time. Gordon
Durie wrapped up a 3-0 win.
Rangers had been
through the mixer but Smith
was once again finding the

spirit to bind his troops
together as his goalkeeper
found the route back from a
personal crisis.

Andy Goram's weight
problems and attitude had
left the manager so fed up in
the summer that he slapped
the stunned No. 1 on the
transfer-list – the shock
treatment worked.

Rather than buckle and
move on, Goram gritted his
teeth and shed the pounds
to blast back into the reck-
oning and win a new four
year deal.

Now he was back where
he belonged and he pulled
off a string of key saves to
build the platform for a 2-0

win at Falkirk on September
17 that featured Boli in the
form that had persuaded
Rangers to shell out £2.7
million for his signature.

The flamboyant French-
man had been the main man
of the Marseille side who
edged the Ibrox side out of
Europe a kick of the ball
away from the final in 1993.

Bernard Tapie's club
were ultimately disgraced
when the crown was
stripped from them in a
bribes scandal but back then
Boli was the cornerstone –
at Rangers he was simply
rocky.

Yet there were flashes of
inspiration at times and at

BRUSH WITH BASILE.. Boli and Cadette get to grips at Brockville

Brockville he bludgeoned home a left-foot shot to give Rangers a flyer before Laudrup curled home a classic free-kick to seal it.

But as he looked back on his debut season Brian confessed: "You couldn't have much more contrast in how I settled here and Boli's problems.

"I think that players from Scandinavia come with a willingness to accept the different cultures of the clubs who pay their wages.

"Basile I felt disappointed a lot of people with his attitude, he couldn't seem to accept the Scottish mentality."

MANY trace the ill-will between Rangers and Aberdeen back to that fateful day in 1988 when Neil Simpson lost all semblance of footballing reason and left Ian Durrant's right knee in tatters.

But in all honesty it has to be said that the feud goes back to the early 80s when Dons boss Alex Ferguson used all the savvy he'd learned as a kid in Govan then as an Ibrox star to return and beat his former favourites on their own patch.

By September 24, 1994, the festering feud had reached a new low and

Hateley was assaulted by a Dons fan in the Pittodrie car park after an explosive 2-2 draw that saw Durie ordered off after the final whistle.

The game ended in fury and farce after Michael Watt picked up a Colin Woodthorpe pass back and Rangers took the free-kick quickly for Hateley to score what would have been the winner.

Ref Les Mottram ordered a retake then blew the final whistle immediately as raging Rangers stars screamed for a handball by Stewart McKimmie after the second effort. Before that mayhem Hateley had netted and Aussie kid Craig Moore grabbed his first goal for the club but Scott Booth and Billy Dodds, a diehard Ibrox fan as a youngster, hauled the Dons level.

The following week against Dundee United at Ibrox Ally McCoist returned for his first outing since the opening day.

But the miserable toll of a broken leg, a hernia operation and a torn calf muscle were to tell on him throughout an injury-scarred season that saw him start just four Premier games.

Hateley and Laudrup got the goals as Light Blues' prospect Charlie Miller lapped up his home league debut – and the Danish Superstar was relishing life beside a player who'd been worshipped at Brian's old club AC Milan.

He stressed: "Mark Hateley is such an interesting player to link up with, so powerful and I felt right away that we were a good mix.

"I'd heard all about the Hateley-McCoist partnership but Ally was injured a lot in my first season and it was down to Mark and I.

"We're very different players but you need that sometimes and we were good for each other, he fed off my crosses.

"I was to score 13 goals

that season but I've always taken more pleasure from creating them and Hateley was a great target to hit."

In the wake of that success, though, Rangers went through a dramatic week that ended with two players cast as Loan Rangers and one big name in the sin bin.

The news that Ian Durrant was off south to Everton on trial alongside £4.1 million striker Duncan Ferguson came as boss Walter Smith reassessed his options for the challenges ahead.

Durrant was to be welcomed back to his spiritual home when doomed Goodison chief Mike Walker decided against the move and disgracefully decided to tell the Ibrox hero his fate while celebrating a rare win in a disco.

But big Dunc was gone, after starting just eight league

games and scoring two Premier goals in 14 fraught months – the big gamble had failed.

On the field there were pitfalls waiting too as Hibs dumped the champs 2-1 at Easter Road with Boli grabbing another goal before being red-carded.

Miller then claimed his first goal for Rangers before a mesmerising Laudrup run allowed the marauding David Robertson to open his account for the season in a 2-0 home win over Kilmarnock. But still there were chinks in the armour and Motherwell's Dougie Arnott exposed them with a double in a 2-1 Fir Park win.

Arnott's one-man mission against Rangers remains one of the Scottish game's great duels, the 5ft

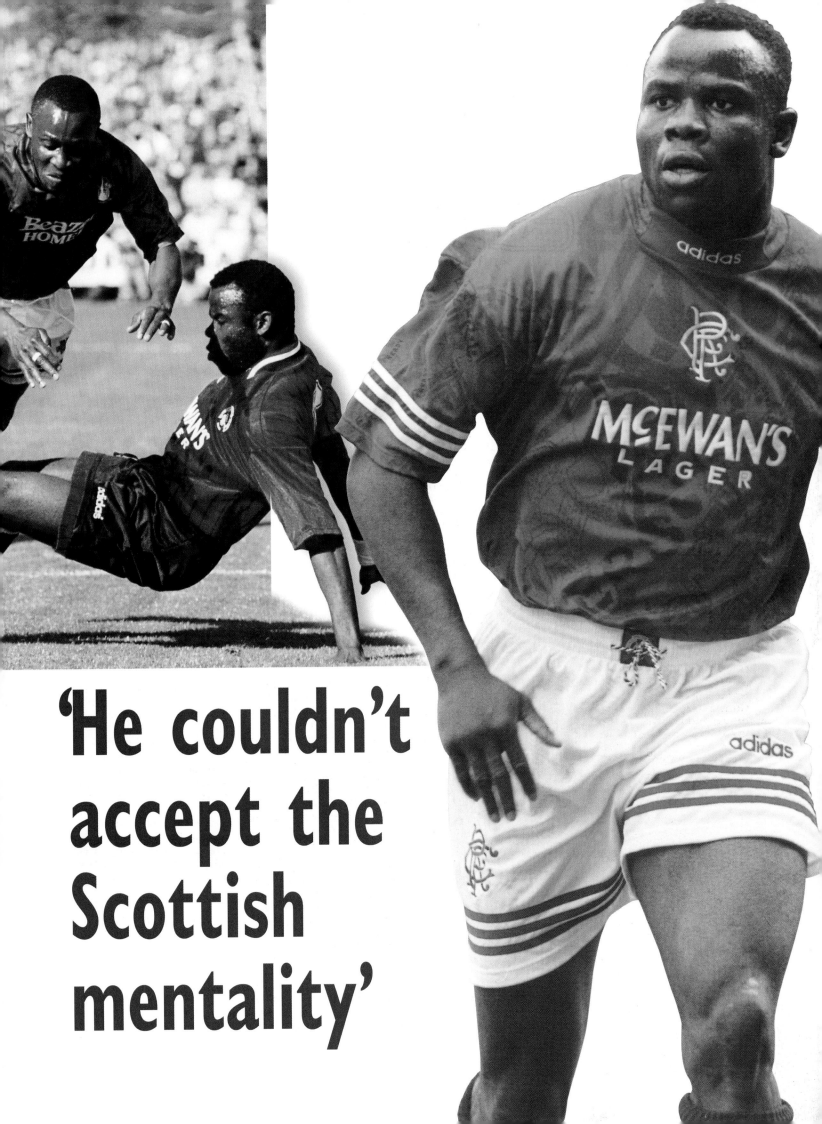

'He couldn't accept the Scottish mentality'

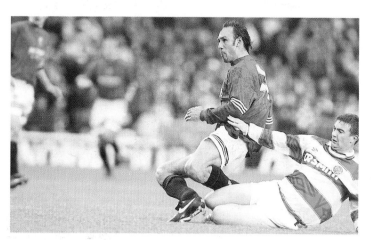

7ins hitman has always seemed to bristle at the mere sight of the Light Blue jerseys.

'Well would come back to Ibrox later that campaign for a 2-0 win when the title race was over and guess who would score one of the goals?

For now, Rangers had to pick themselves up for a crucial Old Firm clash with

added spice as Celtic played the role of lodgers at Hampden with Parkhead under reconstruction.

As the October rain teemed down it was to be an afternoon that Laudrup would store away in his memory banks for the days when he finally does hang up his boots.

Brian accepted his Bell's

Player of the Month award before the match and spent the next 90 minutes showing just why he'd won it.

Miller cunningly ambushed the dithering Tom Boyd to help set up Hateley for a slick sidefoot finish with his weaker right foot.

And although Paul Byrne scored for Celts big Mark netted again to take his haul

against the Hoops to nine goals.

The stage was set for Laudrup to launch on to a long ball and glide away from the trailing Brian O'Neil, a sidestep round Gordon Marshall and he recalled: "Scoring against Celtic at Hampden will always live with me because I had always read about the

'I'll always remember scoring against Celtic at Hampden'

OLD FAVOURITE...
Laudrup loves
facing Celtic and he
relished his first meeting
with them at Hampden as
goals from Hateley (2) and
the Dane sealed a 3-1 win

traditions of that place and the great games that had been played there.

"It was an exciting game and a thrilling goal, running away to go round the keeper and then seeing that net gaping ahead of you – what a feeling!"

The scene of Laudrup, sodden socks at his ankles, leading the Rangers celebra-

tions seemed a lifetime away from the dejected Dane who had trooped off Ibrox an Old Firm fall-guy just two months earlier.

And he pointed out: "It was the first time too that I can say I was able to actually enjoy the old Firm game.

"In my debut I remember the first whistle blowing and then we were trooping off

after losing 2-0, it all just whizzed by me.

"In the seasons after that I was able to warn people like Jocky Bjorklund just what to expect when this crazy game started!"

That day at Hampden also brought a baptism of fire for a long-term Smith signing target.

At the age of just 23, Alan

McLaren of Hearts was hot property after stunning shows for Scotland, shackling world-class stars like Germany's striker Jurgen Klinsmann and Italy's Roberto Baggio.

Now, with Dave McPherson heading the other way to Tynecastle, the £1.25m-rated stopper had the stage he wanted and he

'Laudrup left defenders in his wake'

flourished with a debut to remember.

Laudrup, meanwhile, was to follow up that old firm strike with another in a 3-0 cruise over Partick Thistle before Smith's side stuttered to successive 1-1 draws with Hearts and Falkirk.

Any worries that they were heading for a slump were averted when McCoist bagged what would be his only league goal of a sad season in a 1-0 triumph over Aberdeen.

The dismal Dons were to finish second bottom of the table and require a play-off against Dunfermline to secure their Premier future.

DECEMBER has often been the proving ground for Rangers on this road to Scottish footballing history and 1994 was no different.

Laudrup bagged goals in a sparkling 3-0 success at Dundee United and a 2-0 win at Killie before Hibs went down at Ibrox to set up a milestone match in this seven-in-a-row campaign.

The scene was Fir Park on Hogmanay and Motherwell met a side smarting for revenge after their last visit

to the steel town – with Laudrup inspirational once more – they got it.

Tigerish midfielder Stuart McCall swept Rangers ahead but Paul McGrillen levelled before a Laudrup goal laced with genius and luck.

He left defenders in his wake to curl in a sweet shot that looked a certain scorer until it thumped back off the inside of the post to the dismay of the travelling support behind the goal.

But in a comic moment they were delirious within a split second as the ball careered back and smacked off the head of grounded Well keeper Stevie Woods to roll into the empty net.

It was the spur Rangers needed and Durie made it a Happy New Year, picking the moment perfectly to produce a lightning breakaway and a surefooted finish for his

first strike in three months.

The 3-1 win was to prove hugely significant and Laudrup said: "That win over Motherwell was critical and it's become the time of year when other sides find it very difficult to live with us.

"I remember thinking that if we could win that one we'd be on our way to the title and that's the way it proved."

Now Rangers faced the third Old Firm clash of the season as hot favourites but the Ibrox showdown proved an anti-climax.

Ian Ferguson nabbed what would be the sole goal of a troubled season for him from close range but Byrne once more became the scourge of the Ibrox men with a wonderful back post volley to snatch a point.

Yet Laudrup remained in awe of the spectacle of it all at times, this fevered match that means so much to so many people.

And he sighed: "I always think it's under-estimated, the incredible pulling power of Rangers and Celtic.

"When I was at Milan and Fiorentina you couldn't guarantee a full house every week.

"But at Ibrox and now Parkhead it's a certainty, it's amazing to have two clubs who can do that in a country of just five million people."

Rangers needed a goal from left-back Robertson to secure a point at Partick three days later and they were winding up to say goodbye to a player who had given outstanding value for money.

Pieter Huistra was a shrewd Graeme Souness signing for just £300,000 from FC Twente Enschede back in August 1990.

And five years later he bowed out in the best possible style when the champions travelled to Brockville on a chill January afternoon and left 14 points clear in the title race.

Huistra was bound to be big in Japan's new clash-laden J-League with Hiroshima San Frecce and his farewell was fitting for a player who had grown in stature with every passing season at the club.

The Dutchman rifled home two crackers as McCall grabbed the other in a 3-2 win before saying an emotional goodbye and shaking hands with fans on the way off the pitch.

He left behind moments to cherish, like an extremely rare right-foot finish that helped clinch a crucial

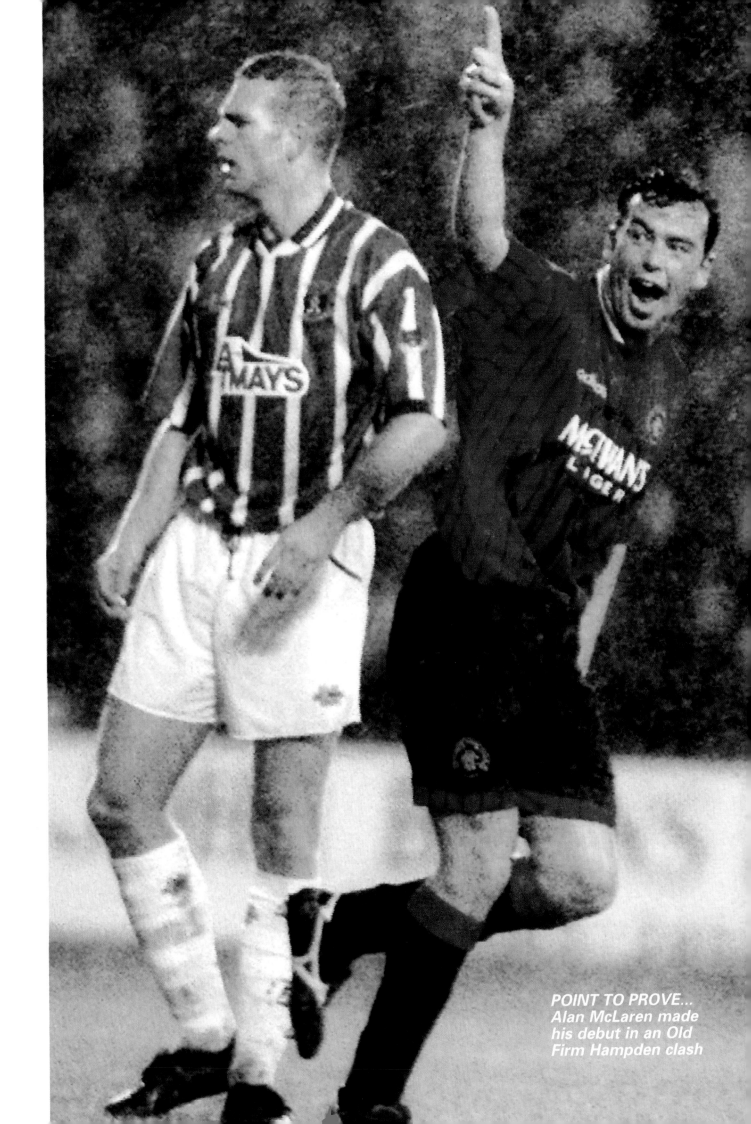

POINT TO PROVE...
Alan McLaren made
his debut in an Old
Firm Hampden clash

EASTERN PROMISE...
Peter Huistra quit Ibrox
for the Japanese league

Champions League point in Bruges after an even more astonishing happening – Ally McCoist actually left the ball to him in the six-yard box!

The developing Miller struck again to edge out Hearts before a 1-1 draw at home to Dundee United set the scene for an unexpected Pittodrie defeat.

Aberdeen were reeling after the departure of boss Willie Miller but the players who had flopped to get him the sack suddenly clicked under Roy Aitken and Dodds and Duncan Shearer sent the champions skidding to defeat.

Boss Smith decided it was time to recharge the batteries and the squad jetted off to Monte Carlo for a break.

It didn't pay off this time as hyped–up Hearts ripped Rangers to pieces to roar home 4-2 in a crunch Tennents Scottish Cup fourth round clash on their return.

But Laudrup believes that some nights on the tiles have helped create a history making squad.

He insisted: "There's nothing wrong with players having a pint or two after they've won. Richard Gough once said the team that drinks together, wins together and I agree.

"I don't mean going on

'A team that drinks together wins together'

binges, I mean laughing together and creating a bond.

"If you've shared something like that it makes you go the extra yard for your mates on the field.

"I may have had a bad time in the Cup against Hearts back then but in 1996 I was to end up drunk on the roof of a team bus with Gazza and the goalie after we beat them 5-1 in the Final."

The sophisticated Dane also believes that it was fellow import Boli's disdain for the Ibrox team spirit that eventually proved to be a big part in his downfall.

Basile had already clashed with boss Smith after criticising his European tactics and described the long-established Rangers practice of players always wearing a collar and tie into training as "stupid".

And Laudrup revealed: "Personally, I've always found the Ibrox dressing room entertaining but Basile never wanted to be part of all that.

"But when people moan about our parties in places like Monaco I refuse to comment because I can't remember them!

"Seriously, in the happy times in my footballing life I

have always found that a team that socialise together will do well.

"We had that at Brondby when Peter Schmeichel, John Jensen and I helped lead the fun after two championship wins and it was great to find the same sort of spirit at Rangers."

The hangover from the Cup defeat was quickly cured with Brian on the mark again in a 3-0 hammering of Kilmarnock before Durie secured a point against his former club Hibs at Easter Road.

Laudrup once more and John Brown were then on target in a surprise home 2-2 draw with Falkirk.

And although Brian netted again at Tynecastle Smith's side slid to their second defeat from the Jambos in the space of a month with John Robertson and John Millar hogging the headlines this time. The headlines, though, were soon to be dominated in far more heartbreaking fashion than the simple loss of a football match.

Davie Cooper left Rangers for Motherwell in August 1989 at the age of 33 with the first title of what was to become this nine-in-a-row run in the bag.

As I've said before in

these pages it remains one of the game's cruellest ironies that the Souness revolution hit Ibrox when Coop was past his 30th birthday. He was tailor-made for the new Rangers.

He had laboured for nine years at Rangers before Souness arrived, part of a tremendous Treble team in 1978 but then for too long surrounded by mediocrity.

For a generation of Gers fans raised on starvation rations, Coop was their reason for going to the football.

Quite simply he was

often the only player the club had worth the admission money.

So although he'd left Ibrox for Fir Park, he was always regarded as The Moody Blue – the man with the magic in his left foot who'd seen 5,000 fans locked out when he had his sell-out testimonial against Bordeaux.

On March 22, 1995 all those memories were sent juddering into awful reality on the news pages of the papers when Davie had a brain haemorrhage while training kids for a TV programme at Clyde's Broadwood Stadium.

He battled through the night but at 9.45am the next morning the life support machine was switched off – unbelievably, Cooper was dead.

WRITING this now takes me back to a phone call to Davie just ten days before he was snatched away.

I was discussing doing an interview with him for the sports pages of the *Sunday Mail*. We agreed to set something up and chatted about football and Laudrup in particular. He raved about him for ten minutes.

Then, as we broke off because he wanted to see how a horse was doing in a race on the telly, he said: "Aye, Laudrup. Some player but he's got nae left foot."

I've never told that story before. It seemed like intruding somehow. I could never claim Coop as a close friend.

He was just someone I admired and was lucky enough to get the chance to talk to a handful of times through my job.

Yet, when he died, I felt this dull aching loss. I can't really begin to comprehend what his family and those close to him suffered.

Ally McCoist was bereft and said: "The feeling in the dressing-room was that we had lost a brother.

"Although he had been away from the club for a while he had never really been away. I don't think he ever will be."

The first chance Rangers had to pay homage to Davie's memory came at Tannadice on April 1 and they did it in style.

Billy Kirkwood had moved from the Ibrox back-room staff to take over the Dundee United hotseat and told his new charges to stay tight against Rangers. They did too, for 12 seconds.

That's how long it took Durie to nick the opener and McLaren cemented a sensational free-kick beyond Kelham O'Hanlon from fully 35 yards to tie it up within eight minutes.

'The feeling was we had lost a brother'

Now the title was agonisingly close and at Ibrox Durrant was back to his devilish best against Aberdeen, scoring and inspiring his side to a 3-2 win.

That paved the way for a title-winning party against Hibs at home on April 16 and goals from Durie, Durrant and Alexei Mikhailitchenko gave Rangers the verdict 3-1.

For Laudrup – touched and deeply flattered to be compared to Cooper throughout his first season – it was a day to savour.

He said: "The day we won the league meant a lot because I'd had my league medals at Brondby and Milan gave me one when I played 14 Serie A games for them but I really earned this one.

"It was a season's hard work and that day, with all your friends and family around you, was so special.

"I'd wanted to prove to Walter Smith that he was right to have faith in me and at the end of the season so many Player of the Year awards came in that I began to think the knighthood might be next – it was an amazing spell.

"But I knew deep down that from that first day against Motherwell I had played the most consistent football of my life."

A faltering end to a long, hard season saw victory at Kilmarnock before 'Well won 2-0 at Ibrox.

Then came a bitterly disappointing 3-0 humbling from Celtic at Hampden that was summed up by a comic cuts own goal from Moore – the good news for Rangers came after.

Paul Gascoigne was on his way from Lazio in a record £4.3million move and another dramatic chapter was about to be written.

A tame 1-1 draw with Partick brought the curtain down and Boli was to bolt for pastures new.

But Laudrup was here to stay and intent on putting a stop to a wandering career.

He confessed: "Much had been made of the fact that I'd never completed a contract before I came to Rangers.

"But I've never regretted the three-year deal I signed and agreeing to another year was easy.

"I will sit down in the summer of 1998 and consider what the future holds for Mette, the kids and I, but until then it will be Rangers."

The magic mantle of the maverick Cooper had flitted through worthy players in Mark Walters and Huistra but it finally found its true successor in Laudrup.

It would have been mouthwatering to see them both in the one team, games would have been stopped specially to give the other side a kick!

Cooper's paltry 22 caps for his country reflect badly on the way genius is judged in this country, Laudrup has never thirsted for plaudits in his homeland.

And still the admiring managers will come his way with Manchester United boss Alex Ferguson a confirmed fan.

He's at Rangers for now, though, and said: "I've sat on the phone in my living room and twice listened to Barcelona asking me to go and play for them, but it doesn't tempt me.

"Other clubs may have their eyes on me but signings like Sebastian Rozental and Jonas Thern encourage me and I feel we finally can make our mark in Europe.

"It's hard for Rangers because of that early round when inevitably there are injuries and new players trying to fit in.

"But we did it in 1993 before I arrived and I'm sure we can do it again."

This chapter is brought to you
in association with

Ho Wong

RESTAURANT

Reborn Gascoigne helps seal number 8

CHAPTER 8

RANGERS' daring in the transfer market has become their hallmark since the Graeme Souness Revolution. But on July 10, 1995 they surpassed the fans' wildest dreams as Paul Gascoigne checked into Ibrox.

At £4.3 million from Italian giants Lazio, Gazza was the costliest signing in the club's history but boss Walter Smith knew he had purchased sheer footballing quality.

He acknowledged the emotional baggage that came with the signing of the temperamental superstar yet he also prized the midfield brilliance he could bring to the team.

There were to be excesses off the park and a Champions League Group of Death without a win hurt Gascoigne but his contribution as Rangers won the title by four points from rejuvenated Celtic was immense.

By the end of it all he'd scored 19 goals and inspired the club to a league and Cup double.

Gazza was everyone's Player of the Year and after all the turmoil of Italy he was to confess: "Walter gave me my life back."

THE life and times of Paul Gascoigne have inspired a mountain of newsprint and hours of TV and radio debate – but one thing remains unsaid.

No-one has ever claimed that Gazza is a bad player.

Rangers knew what they were taking on when they signed the England midfielder and ended his injury-torn Italian stint with Lazio that had turned sour on him.

They knew there would be tantrums and bust-ups surrounding him, there always has been from the days when rival fans threw Mars Bars at the tubby kid starring for Newcastle.

But they also knew that in Gascoigne they had lured a rare talent and on April 28, 1996 at Ibrox he gave the fans a title-clinching afternoon that will go down in Rangers' folklore.

The Ibrox men needed all three points against Aberdeen to secure their eighth title on the trot and they looked to Gazza for inspiration after Brian Irvine had fired the Dons in front.

He drove into the box to plunder a sensational solo goal to level it in the first-half. But with 10 minutes left it seemed certain Walter Smith's side would face a nerve-jangling trip to Kilmarnock on the final day of the season with their championship hopes still hanging in the balance.

Then a drained Gascoigne, his energy sapped by his efforts to steer his team to glory in the heat, got the shout that was to drive him on to the goal of his life.

He recalled frankly: "I was knackered but Alan McLaren looked over and said 'Gazza, do it for us'.

"I was bent double and I said 'I can't, I'm done'. But he kept saying it, telling me

I could do it." And McLaren was right.

Gascoigne took possession in his own half and the adrenalin injected by a roaring Rangers support flowed through him.

He hared off, beating tackles at first by darting skill and then, as he edged nearer the end of a 70-yard run, simply muscling them aside.

It all ended with a left-foot shot that curled beyond Michael Watt to send Ibrox into ecstasy.

Gazza smiled: "All of a sudden I was running and running and then I shot and it was in. It was a magnificent feeling and I nearly

WELCOME ABOARD ... Paul Gascoigne arrives at Glasgow Airport with Walter Smith to kick off his Rangers' career

'I begged Ally to let me hit the penalty'

fainted from exhaustion in the celebrations.

"There were eight other players on top of me before Alan joined them and almost killed me with the extra weight.

"To this day I thank God that Andy Goram didn't bother coming out of his box to join in, then I really would have been dead!"

Gazza had been running on empty but the burning desire was there, the hunger never to waver. In the end he had a feast.

Four minutes from time Durie was hauled down in the box and the penalty brought a heartbreaking decision for sub Ally McCoist.

The striker, out-of-contract in the summer, had a whirl-wind of thoughts spinning around in his head that day.

He had offers to consider and he feared this would be his last goal for the club. But close pal Gascoigne was on a hat-trick as he sought the first championship medal of his career.

And Paul revealed: "When we got the penalty I BEGGED Ally to let me take it.

"It would be my first hat-trick for Rangers on the day we won the league and I reminded him he'd already scored loads of hat-tricks for the club."

McCoist didn't give up without a fight and tried to reason with the Englishman before reluctantly tossing the ball across.

And Gazza, delighted to see McCoist turn down Japanese side Shimuzu S-Pulse, Yanks Kansas City Wizards and Swiss club Servette to sign a new two-year Rangers deal that summer, admitted: "Ally was scared that this was his last game and his last chance for Rangers.

"But it's a hard life and I just said 'Oh well, if you're leaving **** off, I'm taking it'."

Gazza duly converted the kick to clinch a 3-1 win.

Behind the smiles, it was a day when you saw inside the heart of a man often painted as a superstar tormented by personal demons.

All the demands, all the pressures of the fame he often can't cope with slip away from Gascoigne on a football pitch. It's his escape.

Who could forget that five years earlier he'd played for Spurs in the 1991 FA Cup final and put his golden future at risk with a scandalously violent challenge on Nottingham Forest's Gary Charles that wrecked his own knee.

For a player so often man-marked and booted from pillar to post there was a bitter irony that his career-threatening injury should be self-inflicted.

But now after all the dark days and the pain that followed, he was a hero again.

He burst into tears hugging Gordan Petric on the sidelines and then was hoisted aloft by his Rangers team-mates clutching the match ball as a prize for his hat-trick.

And he said: "I've had 15 operations and I've worked hard to get back from every one. But I remember that day I thought about other players

WAVES OF HYSTERIA ... fans flocked to Ibrox to greet Gazza and the player took it all in his stride

who've had to quit and thought how fortunate I was.

"I still look back at that tackle against Forest and think that if I hadn't launched into that then I'd have been all right.

"I daren't think too much about that, though, because it would do my head in.

"I just handed my FA Cup medal to my mum and told her to keep it.

"Now after all the ops and all the heartache I had my first championship medal with Rangers – believe me, I kept that one."

Although lauded by the Lazio fans, Gascoigne had never had a chance to show his true form in Italy as his injury jinx haunted him.

Increasingly, he felt an English media that created the Gascoigne phenomenon

after Italia '90 had turned on him.

But in that first season in Scotland he once more turned the tap on the talent that had always marked him out as unique.

He was the PFA Player of the Year and the choice of the Scottish Football Writers' Association.

GAZZA reflected: "I'd scored 19 goals in the season and I was proud and pleased to be with a bunch of players who had made me as relaxed as I'd been since my time at Newcastle.

"I won about 30 Player of the Year awards that season and any time I'm low I just

'I just told him that I'm signing'

go into the trophy room and look at them and think: "Yep, that's what football is all about."

Rangers 3, Aberdeen 1. It had been the final chapter in a dramatic title story that began in a summer that also saw manager Smith boost his resources with three further signings.

Long-time target Stephen Wright, who was to be tragically seriously injured in a Champions League clash against Juventus with his Ibrox career in its infancy, made the switch from Aberdeen.

And Smith dashed from Rangers' pre-season camp in Denmark to thwart Celtic and scoop stopper Gordan Petric from his old club Dundee United in a £1.5m transfer.

He was later to tie up Russian striker Oleg Salenko, a player who could never grasp the camaraderie that unites the Ibrox dressing room.

Salenko would be quickly jettisoned despite a reasonable record of seven goals in 16 games.

MEANWHILE, Gascoigne knew his Serie A adventure was coming to a close when Lazio's owner Sergio Cragnotti and coach Dino Zoff flew to London in a bid to find a buyer for the mercurial midfielder.

He demanded talks when they returned to Rome and he revealed: "You know, peo-

ple said I had problems with Zoff but that wasn't true. He was a great man and he remains a friend to this day.

"But I had to know what was happening for my future and I asked him straight out who wanted me.

"He told me 'Chelsea, Aston Villa, Sheffield Wednesday and Rangers.

"I said 'no, I'm not interested in any of them'.

"Then he went on and said he thought I might have fancied the chance of a move to Glasgow.

"I thought it was Queens Park Rangers he'd been talking about and when the mix-up was cleared up I told him to get Rangers on the phone right away."

Smith jetted to Rome the next day and held the most bizarre signing talks of his

life in the grounds of Gascoigne's luxury villa.

Paul smiled: "When he arrived I was doing weights on the patio. At that time I was down to 11st 5lbs which was really too thin but I hoped he'd be impressed by my fitness.

"I welcomed Walter and asked my mate Jimmy to get us two beers and the Gaffer just looked at me.

"We settled with the beers and he said 'let me tell you about the club'.

"I just stopped him in mid-sentence and told him 'I'm signing'."

The deal was the biggest shock to hit Scottish football since Mo Johnston checked into Ibrox six years earlier.

But Gascoigne had been impressed by Smith ever since he brought his own supply of beer to a Florida beach in 1993!

Gazza recalled: "It was only because he was a typical canny Scotsman that we got talking in the first place on holiday.

"There was this 200-yard walk to the beach to the bar to get a drink and by the time you were back at your towel whatever you'd bought was warm.

"Then all of a sudden two kids came on the beach with this cool-box the size of a juggernaut filled with beer.

"So I went over and started chatting, stole a couple of beers and played football with Walter's sons and that's how we got talking.

"I said to my Sheryl then 'that's the manager of Rangers Football Club'. She said 'Oh, are they big?'

"I replied 'they're massive, I'd love to sign for them'. Two years later I did."

Gascoigne had sought the advice of Ray Wilkins, Terry Butcher and Chris Woods before the talks with Smith

'Rangers had two geniuses on the staff'

that brought him to Glasgow.

Their verdict had been unanimous: Sign and you'll never regret it.

He swept into Scotland after helping England beat Japan 2-1 in an Umbro Cup clash at Wembley and was astounded to find out that 1000 Rangers fans knew all about his "top secret" flight.

When all the hype and glamour of his arrival finally died down, Gazza had the chance to settle into his new club on a pre-season tour of Denmark.

Rangers now had two vastly different geniuses on the staff – the flamboyant Gascoigne and family man Brian Laudrup really were the Odd Couple.

Covering that tour, I was privileged enough to sit on a hillside in the sun on those mornings in the sleepy village of Ebeltoft and watch them test each other's abilities to the limit in training matches.

Gascoigne had been the most gifted player at every club he'd played for, now he had an equal.

He said: "I was intrigued to meet Laudrup because he had suffered

the same as me in Italy, he couldn't relax and enjoy his football.

"In training he was just unbelievable and at the start I was trying to outdo him.

"We'd end up going for nutmegs against each other but I stopped it when I beat him and he smashed me from behind. I learned to behave after that."

Back home to the serious business of building up for the season and Gazza joked his way into his first storm, imitating playing the flute after scoring in a 4-0 Ibrox International Tournament win over Steaua Bucharest.

Duped by team-mates to do it, he was pilloried for his antics and it was clear he would have to learn some quick lessons about life in the bitterly-divided city of Glasgow.

On the field he scored on his competitive home debut as Morton were seen off in the Coca-Cola Cup and he helped Rangers edge past Anorthosis Famagusta of Cyprus to make the cash-rich Champions League.

Rangers started the league season steadily with three clean sheets and three wins over Kilmarnock, Raith and Falkirk.

But a 1-0 Euro defeat from Steaua got them off to a dismal start and Darren Jackson gave Hibs a shock Ibrox win in the first league setback. There were grim

WRIGHT CARRY-ON ... Gazza and Ian Wright have a laugh on England duty

NO FAL-TERING …
Alan McLaren
wins this challenge
with Falkirk's Mo
Johnston as
another league
win is clocked up

warnings for Smith's side over their fate when German cracks Borussia Dortmund flew into town but Gascoigne chose that night to produce his best display yet in a Rangers jersey.

Twice the Bundesliga giants led through Heiko Herrlich and Martin Kree but twice the defiant Gazza hauled Rangers back into it as he set up equalisers for Richard Gough and Ian Ferguson.

Now the stage was set for his league debut in the game that – rightly or wrongly – means more to a Rangers fan than any other.

Eleven days earlier a McCoist back post header from Gazza's cross had dismantled Celts in the last eight of the Coca-Cola Cup.

Now Rangers were back on the old enemy's turf and Gascoigne, a ball of twitching energy at the best of times, felt caged in the Parkhead dressing-room with butterflies dancing in his stomach as he waited for kick-off.

FINALLY he could take no more and he revealed: "I was so nervous before that game that when I was in my strip I just walked into the bar in the lounge and said: "Double whisky, please.

"I knocked it back, the tension was gone and I went on to score.

"It happened again when we came to the Coca-Cola Cup final with Hearts at Parkhead the following season.

"I'd had a scuffle with Ally McCoist on the park and the dressing room atmosphere wasn't too good.

"So I thought that's it, I'm going to do the same as I did against Celtic.

"I went back in, knocked back a double and after the break I scored two and we won the cup.

"Right enough, Andy Goram did tell me to go and have one before another Old Firm game and I missed a

DERBY DAZE ... Gascoigne goes bananas after scoring his first goal against Celtic

'My first league goal for clubs is always in derbies'

penalty – so it doesn't always work."

In the latest Old Firm battle, the vastly under-rated Alex Cleland had set Rangers on their way with a skidding header that was to prove his only league goal of the season.

Then Gascoigne steamed forward on a searching 70-yard run into the heart of Celtic's defence to get on the end of Ally McCoist's wonderfully judged pass.

The clip over Gordon Marshall was perfection and he said: "The feeling when you score against Celtic and run to the Rangers End is indescribable, you would have to do it yourself to appreciate it.

"But no-one should have been surprised. My first game for Newcastle was the derby against Sunderland then I made my derby debut for Spurs against Arsenal and

scored after my boot flew off. Then I went to Lazio and scored a header against Roma that I'll never forget, it was my first goal for the club.

"So it was fated that my first league goal for Rangers would be against Celtic.

"Everywhere I've gone my first league goal has been in derbies."

Gazza followed that strike with another in the 2-1 win over Motherwell four days later but picked up a damaging thigh strain that put him in cold storage for a fortnight.

On October 12 the football world was rocked when for-

mer Rangers striker Duncan Ferguson was sent to Barlinnie for his head-butt on Raith's John McStay 18 months earlier.

A month later the long arm of the law was to threaten Gascoigne too after another explosive game with Aberdeen.

The star had to kick his heels in frustration as Craig Moore's back post header snatched a win at Pittodrie before Gordon Durie, in the best form of his Rangers' career, engineered a hat-trick in a 4-0 drubbing of Partick.

Then the sick Geordie

had to watch a footballing murder in Turin as Juventus twisted the knife in a 4-1 thumping that saw Cleland red-carded for a wild kick at the brilliant Alessandro del Piero.

After Italy, the whole club needed a lift and Gazza provided it with a first minute strike against Hearts in a 4-1 romp.

Yet Smith's side flopped 2-2 away to Raith before Gascoigne was given a stinging reminder of just who was in charge at Ibrox.

Before a home clash with Falkirk, the midfielder's life was in turmoil and he chose the wrong way to try and solve those problems.

He said: "I remember I had a lot of personal stuff going on and I was under a lot of pressure.

"I couldn't handle it and I had a couple of pints on the

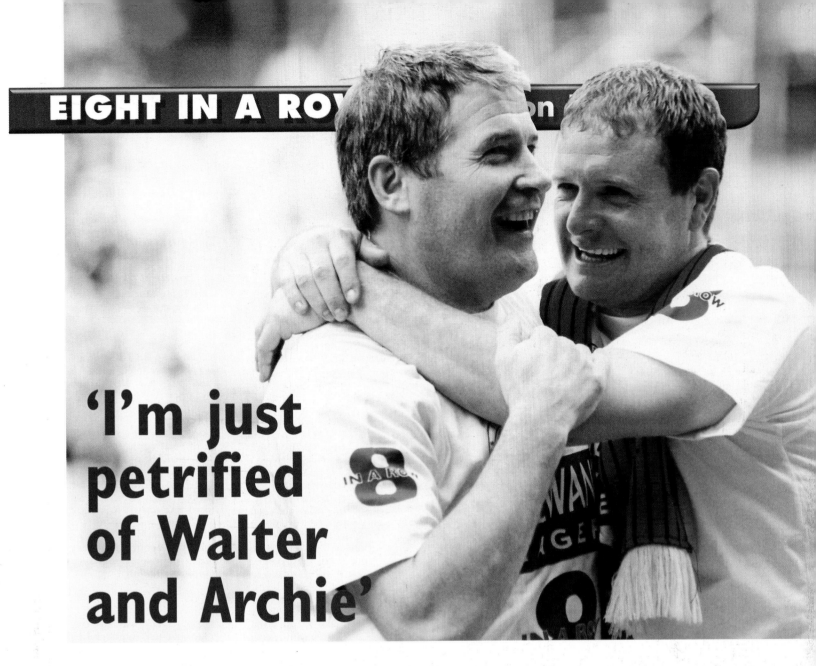

'I'm just petrified of Walter and Archie'

Friday night to unwind.

"Before the game the manager said to me 'what did you do last night'?

"I said I had a couple of pints, Gaffer, that was it – just to relax.

"He said 'okay, then' and he just winked at me."

Gascoigne continued to get ready and was prepared to pull his famous No.8 jersey over his head when assistant boss Archie Knox said: "The Gaffer wants to see you – NOW."

What followed was the short, sharp shock treatment. Paul Gascoigne, international superstar, learned one of the most humiliating lessons of his life.

As we sat in a Glasgow gym talking over his first Ibrox season, Gazza grimaced as he recalled: "I had half my kit on and I went into his room and he said 'go along to that dressing-room and get your suit on and find a seat in the stand'.

"'You are NOT playing for Rangers today'.

"I pleaded my case that I'd been under pressure and he shut me up quick.

"I was told in no uncertain terms that no-one takes the mickey out of him or Rangers and I had overstepped the mark.

"I was absolutely devastated and when I went back to the dressing-room to put

my suit on the lads didn't know whether to laugh at me or be serious.

"You've asked me if I respect Walter Smith, well I don't respect him I'm just PETRIFIED of him. Seriously, Walter and Archie Knox are the only men I'm physically scared of.

"When the manager walks in after a defeat there's silence – you could hear a pin drop.

"And if we're 1-0 down with 10 minutes to go I'm looking at the clock and praying we'll score and go on to win so we don't have to face him.

"It was after that warning that I knew I had to knuckle down."

But trouble was still brewing for Gascoigne before he got his mind straight and became the player who walked away with every

plaudit in May.

Europe was becoming a nightmare now and Juve rubbed salt in the wounds in a 4-0 Ibrox triumph.

Then on November 11 – just 17 days after they'd dumped Rangers out of the Coca-Cola Cup semi-final, arch rivals Aberdeen came to Glasgow and in the midst of one of the most exciting games of the season Gazza walked a knife-edge.

He'd taken a battering in that 2-1 Hampden defeat and it was a day of vengeance and vendettas.

Gascoigne was involved in two unsavoury clashes with Stewart McKimmie and Paul Bernard before appearing to rear into a head-butt that struck John Inglis in the chest and felled the Dons defender.

Ref John Rowbotham's failure to book Gazza that

FEELING THE
STRAIN ... it was
a season of ups
and downs for
Gascoigne

day derailed a promising rise and the repercussions didn't stop there.

The Procurator Fiscal demanded a report and Paul confessed: "I was wired up because it was a huge game.

"I had a scuffle with John Inglis but I couldn't believe the backlash with the threat of the police involved.

"It meant a lot to me at the end of that season when we were in the hotel after we'd beaten them to win the league and John sent over a bottle of champagne for me as a present.

"Since that incident we've been friends and he always told me he didn't hold a grudge and had just felt it was part and parcel of the game."

Eight days later as the legal row raged on, Gazza faced the ultimate test of his temperament against Celtic and Smith stuck by his man.

He was rewarded with one of the player's most mature displays in a light blue jersey despite an early booking for a foul on Jackie McNamara.

The nation's eyes were on him throughout a thrilling 3-3 draw as Andreas Thom rifled Celtic in front before an incredible episode when David Robertson appeared to equalise.

Robbo's strike was ruled offside but amid the celebrations and the confusion that followed the stadium scoreboard still read 1-1 and STV even continued hailing it as a "goal" for 15 minutes.

Laudrup settled the arguments to equalise but John Collins put Celts in front from the spot before Gascoigne's wicked free-kick was glanced home by McCoist.

Tosh McKinlay bundled home a catastrophic near post own goal for the Hoops but Pierre van Hooijdonk's classic header tied it up.

The snap and the snarl that had soured the game for a week after that Dons dust-up was gone as the Old Firm put a smile back on the face of soccer.

And Gazza was grinning, too, in midweek, with the tongue poking out cheekily and the hands clasped above his head in celebration after he raced from the halfway line to carve out another sensational goal at home to Steaua.

Sadly, Adrian Ilie's goal denied Gers even the crumb of comfort of a Euro victory.

PAUL was staying well in check but after a 4-1 win against Hibs and another stunning goal in a 2-0 win at Hearts, he snapped.

Ironically, his moment of madness came on the day the Procurator Fiscal dropped any action against him and he was reported to the SFA for pinching Hearts striker Alan Lawrence on the BOTTOM.

Gazza blew a gasket as Rangers fought to restore some vestiges of pride in Europe in Dortmund.

Booked for a first-half kick at Andreas Moller, Gazza – who had shone in a 2-2 draw in the Westfalenstadion – let off a volley of abuse at Spanish ref Manuel Diaz Vega. With 16 minutes left he was off.

Gascoigne v The Man in Black was to become a regular movie on a TV screen near you in that month of December.

He insisted: "My discipline

'I have had nine bookings for nothing'

is something that's always been questioned but look at the facts.

"I think I had two red cards at Spurs, none at Lazio and for England I've been booked twice in 46 games.

"I've been sent off twice in Europe for Rangers which I bitterly regret but never in the league.

"I also have nine bookings in Scotland that I consider to have been for NOTHING."

As the storm clouds gathered over their most controversial star, there was still the business of winning a league title for Rangers to deal with.

Lifelong fan Derek McInnes, a £400,000 signing from Morton, made his debut as the valuable Durie downed Partick at Ibrox.

A 0-0 draw at Motherwell was then followed by a Gazza-inspired 3-0 win over Kilmarnock.

Spurred on by the sackload of stick, the enigmatic playmaker was thriving

once more and sadly the next showcase of his talents was spoiled by one of the crassest acts of refereeing stupidity you're ever likely to see.

Hibs came to Ibrox on December 30 planning to make a point their prisoner – instead they were executed.

Durie rattled home an astonishing four goals, Charlie Miller and Salenko chipped in and Gazza supplied the coup de grace with an amazing solo strike.

Yet still we were left talking about the Rangers star's battle with officialdom after he BOOKED ref Dougie Smith!

Paul explained: "The ref had dropped his card and I picked it up and kept it because we were on the

attack. When the move broke down I went back to give him it back and booked him for a laugh.

"He actually looked for his to book me because he thought I'd brought my own on the park with me.

"Then he booked me and I couldn't believe it. It didn't sicken me off because I just felt embarrassed for him.

"He must have been embarrassed for himself afterwards.

"Players

and refs are under a lot of pressure these days but surely you can have some fun?"

Ref Jim McGilvray didn't think so. In fact, his decision to book Gascoigne a month later led to him quitting.

Wary of an observer in the stand and hamstrung by new edicts, fed-up McGilvray followed the letter of the law and yellow-carded Gazza for jumping the hoardings

SLIDE RULER ... Gascoigne beats Neil Berry to net against Hearts

'Referees will never destroy me'

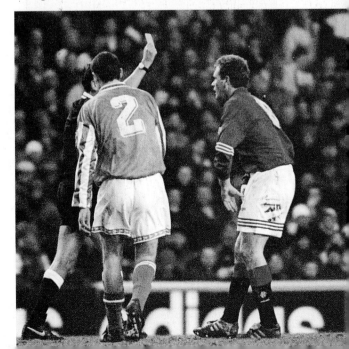

FALLEN HERO ... Gascoigne troops off after his red card against Borussia in Germany

to celebrate after he slammed the second of two belters in a 2-1 win.

The Ibrox idol groaned: "I'd been getting the fatty taunts all day so I made a big belly gesture and jumped back on the pitch and I was booked again.

"I mean what have you done wrong there? I hadn't smashed anyone in the face and I hadn't given anyone the V-sign.

"I was getting the feeling that they were going out to do it so they could go back to the pub that night and tell their mates 'I booked Gazza today'.

"They can carry on doing that if they want but they will never destroy me."

January 3 brought another critical Old Firm clash, with Celtic once more scenting the chance to wrest Rangers' grip on the title.

The 0-0 draw was built on two of the rocks Smith has come to rely on in his hours of need.

Andy Goram snaked out a hand to divert a Phil O'Donnell screamer against the post and Richard Gough was at his inspirational best in defence.

Gough, in fact, will look back on this season and reflect that he would have pushed team-mate Gazza for the Player of the Year award if it hadn't been for two months out injured.

Smith's side then cruised to wins over Falkirk and Raith Rovers – with Brazilian signing target Jardel and supermodel wife Karen watching from the stand – before they were left in the spell of Magic.

Hearts' Allan Johnston won that nickname because his ball skills reminded his mates of the basketball legend.

And the prospect who was later to move to French side Rennes and then return to Britain with Sunderland wove some spells with a hat-trick that day as a bewitched Rangers rearguard were cut to ribbons in a 3-0 humbling.

It was a defeat that called for the response of champions and once more Smith got it.

FOUR straight wins were racked up against Thistle, Well, Aberdeen and Hibs before a March 17 confrontation with Celts that was billed as a title decider.

The tension grew in the build-up and Gascoigne couldn't share his views on the game with a room-mate at Rangers' hideaway hotel – because no-one will share with him.

He admitted: "It's the job at the club that no-one wants. I sleep with the light on and the TV on because it's like having company with me.

"Lately I have the light on, the TV on and headphones on my ears to help me drop off to sleep.

"It works all right, the only problem is I wake up and think I'm a pop star!"

Whatever you may think of Paul Gascoigne the personality, Paul Gascoigne the footballer IS a dedicated professional at work.

Delivering the whipping, impossible to defend crosses he

YELLOW FEVER ... Gazza jokingly books ref Dougie Smith but can't believe the response

'I love football – it's what I live for'

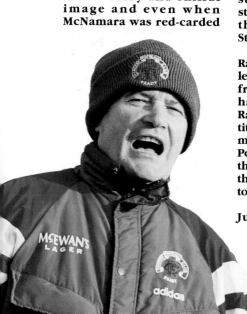

rips in takes practice. Hours of it.

But it pays off in the most taxing arenas and it did that day with a vicious ball that required only a brush off Alan McLaren's forelock to take it into the far corner just before the break.

But this was a Celtic side moulded in boss Tommy Burns' fiery and skilful image and even when McNamara was red-carded they grabbed a draw thanks to never-say-die John Hughes' last gasp header.

Gazza then struck in a scrambled 3-2 win over Falkirk before the club owed one more big debt to McCoist.

Super Ally had an injury-interrupted season that term yet he still managed a superb 16 goals in just 18 starts and none more crucial than those he bagged at Stark's Park on March 30.

Gers were 2-1 down to Raith with just seven minutes left despite a penalty strike from McCoist in the first-half that had marked 300 Rangers goals in all competitions. But when it mattered most the man they call the Polecat seized on his prey in the box to notch a hat-trick then hand a second penalty to Durie.

The reason? He wanted Jukebox to win a £50 bet with Gascoigne over who would score the most goals!

Gascoigne, though, knows that hapless Gordon was the victim of one of THE most memorable wind-ups in a dressing-room famed for them.

HE revealed: "I caught two big trout on one of my fishing expeditions and brought them into Ibrox.

"Coisty said I should take them to the hotel and the chef would cook them for the team.

"So in the morning Ally had Jukey's car to drive us in and I couldn't resist it.

"I lifted the back seat and after about five minutes wrestling I finally jammed the tail of the trout under it – that was one gone.

"Then I lifted the carpet and put the second trout where the spare wheel is. The smell was unbelievable.

"Four or five days later Durie was still coming in and saying there was something wrong with his car!"

The striker was green at the gills every time he got behind the wheel and, by now, was naturally gutted at the state of his club Honda.

And Gazza grinned: "He finally twigged someone had done something and hauled the fish out of the boot not knowing there was still another one left.

"He had the car valeted, he sprayed it and still it wouldn't go away.

"Then Fergie and John Brown borrowed the car from Gordon and they were driving around with the windows open to kill the stench.

"Fergie couldn't under-

stand why the car was stinking every time he stopped at traffic lights.

"Eventually, Jukey found the second trout and he had to give the car back to Honda, they couldn't sell it!"

Eight days after McCoist pulled Rangers out of the wrecker's yard in Fife, the stage was far more glamourous – the Tennents Scottish Cup semi-final with Celtic at Hampden.

It was an afternoon for men with bottle and Gers diehard Brown was back in the fray and commanding as Ally snapped up a rebound from a Robertson shot to roll his side in front.

Laudrup sped away on a Gascoigne pass to lob home a clinical second and Celts – despite van Hooijdonk's consolation goal – were dead and buried.

The title run-in began with a glitch, a 2-0 reverse at Hearts that the Jambos were to pay for come cup final day.

But after that it was cruise control to No.8 for Smith's side with Danish new boy Erik Bo Andersen, who was to score six goals in six starts in the closing games, claiming a hat-trick in a 5-0 annihilation of Partick.

Gascoigne netted once more in a 3-1 win at Motherwell before that triumph over the Dons sealed it.

D URIE'S season ended in personal glory with a double in a 3-0 closing league win at Killie, signalling that he would carry his shooting boots to Hampden for the Final on May 18.

So it proved as Laudrup orchestrated 90 minutes of champagne football to seal the double, scoring twice and helping create a hat-trick for Jukebox.

It was over and Gascoigne savoured it all, a winner again after a season that had taken him through every emotion.

No player in Scottish football history has ever come under such scrutiny yet he remains an enigma.

There have been incidents in his personal life that are indefensible but every time I have sat and talked football with him I walk away thinking he's a gem of a fella.

Every newspaper in the land has had Gazza On the Couch and claimed to be Inside His Mind.

But really it's simple, he's just a working class guy who happens to be a genius at football and it's given him a level of fame he can't handle.

When he leaves, Ibrox debate will rage on whether he was good for the club.

Well, he has scored goals the fans will remember for the rest of their lives and played a major role in two title wins and two cup triumphs.

The last £4m gamble Rangers took played 14 games and ended up in the nick.

Before I left the gym that day Gazza fidgeted nervously with the zip of his Rangers training jacket and said: "I will leave Rangers when Walter Smith and David Murray decide they don't want me or the minute the fans turn against me.

"I won't stay where I'm not wanted, that's for sure. "The pitch is still the only place that I can escape from the pressure.

"I love the game, it's what I live for. All I want to do is play."

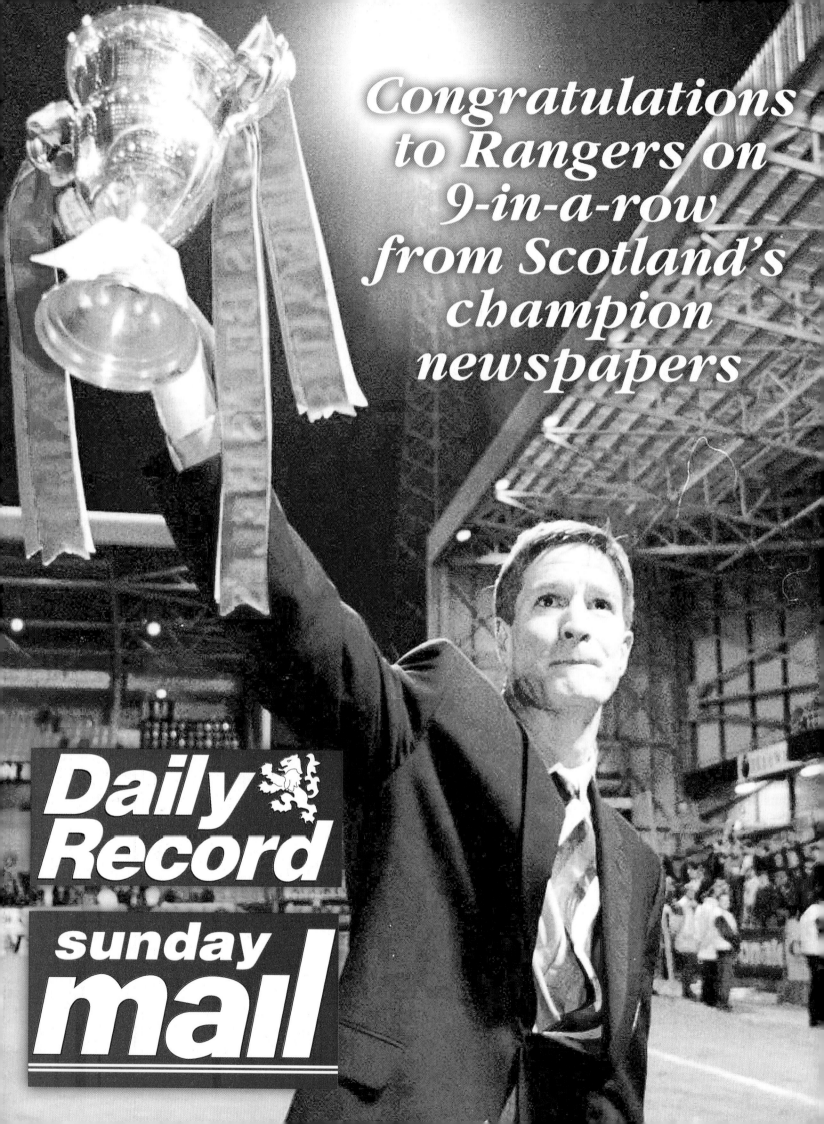

you can always judge a company...

...by the company it keeps

First Press PUBLISHING

Publishers of Slater Hogg & Howison and TSB Property Services Magazine, Miller Homes house styles, Herald property, Rangers News and the programme of The Gulfstream World Invitational Golf Championship at Loch Lomond.

NINE IN A ROW Scottish Premier D

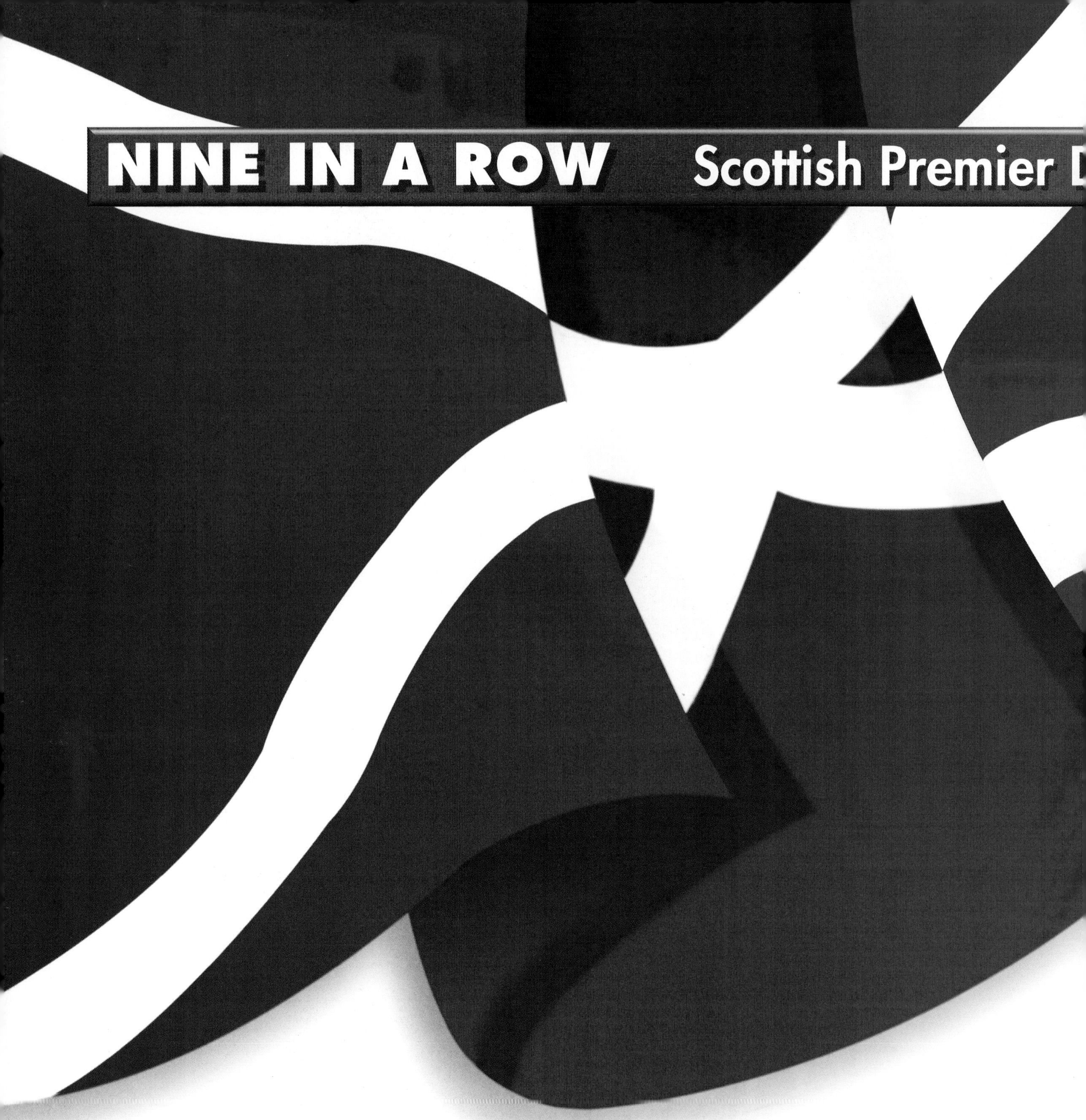

This chapter is brought to you
in association with

**BRITISH
PRINTING
COMPANY**

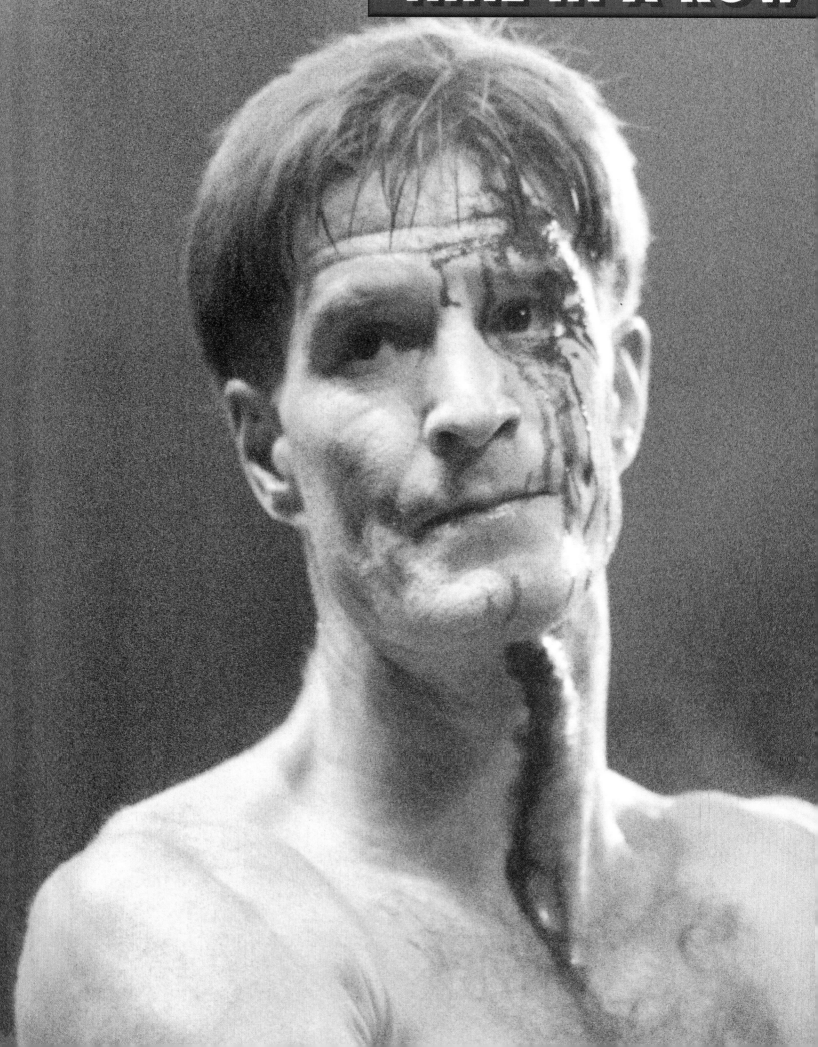

Lionheart goes out at the top

IT was now or never – Rangers had arrived at their date with destiny. The nine-in-a-row run of Jock Stein's Celtic legends had long been a trump card for Hoops fans in any Old Firm argument.

Now the champions were on the brink of matching it and, as the footballing feat became an obsession in Glasgow, it was Walter Smith's side who had the bottle for the battle. Four crunch clashes with their city rivals and four wins brought the first Premier League Grand Slam and those 12 priceless points put Coca-Cola Cup winning Rangers on course.

For once, disappointment in Europe and even a Scottish Cup defeat by Celts could be tolerated. Rangers, inspired by skipper Richard Gough, had written themselves into the history books.

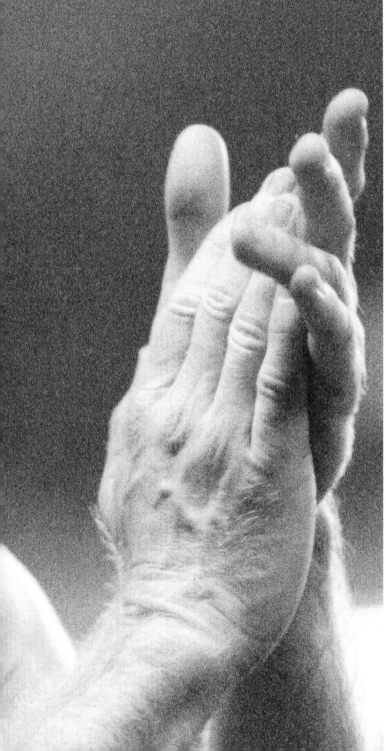

TWO legends sat behind the scenes at Ajax's awesome new Amsterdam Arena and discussed the future for Rangers and AC Milan without them.

Richard Gough and Franco Baresi needed an interpreter to put their views across as a star-studded six-a-side tournament raged on. But, on the field, they'd always spoken the same language.

Gough sat fascinated as he listened to the ageing Italian superstar he has always admired and told Baresi of his decision to quit the club he loves for a new challenge in America.

The Rangers captain, then approaching his 35th birthday, was concerned that, if he stayed any longer, he risked falling from grace at Ibrox.

His pride would not allow it and the news that he'd been allowed to leave for Kansas City Wizards with a year of his contract to run had shocked the Rangers fans.

But in April, as he prepared to return from a calf injury for the run-in to nine-in-a-row, Gough watched the cruel end to Baresi's glittering career at the San Siro. Juventus dismantled his side as they roared to a 6-1 triumph and then Baresi was substituted at half-time in a 3-1 derby defeat from Inter.

At the age of 37 and with coach Arrigo Saachi clinging to memories of his defender's former greatness, Franco had been stripped of his dignity and shorn of his footballing pride.

It was exactly the scenario Gough had feared for himself at Ibrox. That's why he chose to bow out at the end of this most dramatic of seasons.

And taking his final curtain as the man who led Rangers to nine-in-a-row was no more than the lion-hearted captain deserved.

He said: "I've had a great ten years. It's time for young blood to come in.

"Franco Baresi was, for me, the example of what I was scared of. He was now playing in an AC Milan team when he shouldn't have been.

"He was 37, just off the pace, and they were losing games like 6-1 to Juventus.

"Walter Smith was at that game and told me he was just a yard away from everything. Archie Knox noticed the same thing when they lost 3-1 to

'Perhaps you need to take the decision out of the manager's hands ... that's what I've done with Walter'

Inter. He was taken off at half-time in that one and I can imagine how he would feel – he'd feel like shooting himself.

"It would be a terrible blow for a man of his standing, a man with his pride, to suffer that."

That time shared with Baresi in Amsterdam stuck with Gough throughout this momentous season.

And he used it as the conclusive evidence that, hard as it was, he was making the right decision to walk away from the place that had been his life for a decade.

Richard pointed out: "Baresi has won everything and he's done everything.

"So I'm sure he knew he wasn't right, yet the manager still wanted him there.

"Perhaps you need to take the decision out of the manager's hands and that's what I've done with Walter.

"Franz Beckenbauer was my hero as a kid and Baresi was cut from the same cloth, a guy I looked up to who was a similar age to me and

captain of a huge club. Sure, he was at a higher level than me because they were the kings of Europe.

"But he was also such a proud man and had the image of a gentleman. Yet he was a villain on the park, I like that.

"He was very interested in my decision to go to America and admitted he was considering it himself, but Milan were insistent on him being a coach there."

That meeting with the man who had been the rock of Italy's defence came in January, three months after Gough broke the news of his Ibrox departure.

And he was in charge of a side who had ridden a

rollercoaster of emotions right from the season's curtain-raiser against Russian champs Alania Vladikavkaz on August 7.

Walter Smith's summer budget had once more been spent on the continent as he shelled out a total of £5.5million to bring midfielder Jorg Albertz from SV Hamburg and Swedish international defender Joachim Bjorklund from Italian side Vicenza.

By the end of an impressive first season in their new surroundings they would simply be known as The Hammer and Jocky, a vital part of a title team.

Albertz, famed for his thunderbolt freekicks and spectacular goals, caught a tough break as he tried to settle in, with Smith forced to shuttle him to left-back to deputise for the crocked David Robertson.

But the new boys were calm and efficient as Rangers recovered from

being 1-0 down at the break to stride to a 3-1 first-leg lead.

The equaliser that lifted the gloom was just reward for boyhood Rangers fan Derek McInnes, who had fought back from a horrific knee injury at Morton to win the move he'd always craved.

Ally McCoist and Gordan Petric – who stripped off his shirt for some *Simply the Vest* celebrations – wrapped it up but Alania's Igor Yanovsky missed what could have been a costly penalty.

THE nerves were still bared in the league opener at home to Raith Rovers when only a Trevor Steven goal gave the champs all three points.

The shackles, though, came off at East End Park as newly-promoted Dunfermline found out to their cost that they were playing with the big boys

GUNNERS GUNNED DOWN... *Jorg Albertz hits the ball harder than any other player in Britain*

now. McCoist, prematurely written off by many pundits, gorged himself on a hat-trick and then transformed Peter van Vossen grabbed a double in a 5-2 win to set Smith's side up for the Russian return.

It was to be a match that will go down in the club's history books as they raced to an unbelievable 7-2 second leg win.

McCoist floated home a header for the opener within the first 60 seconds and bagged yet another treble with two from Brian Laudrup and goals from van Vossen and Charlie Miller completing a quite astonishing scoreline.

Amid the euphoria, Gough, as ever, remained the cold-eyed professional.

And he reflected: "I have to be honest and say that Vladikavkaz chucked it when they went 3-1 down in the second leg.

"We won 7-2 which was incredible but although they still attacked when they went behind they'd given up the ghost at the back."

Back home on the Saturday Dundee United proved a far tougher obstacle but Paul Gascoigne, even when he's out of touch and half-fit, has the repertoire to out-fox any defence.

This time he jinked inside, then outside in the depths of a sea of tangerine jerseys before curling a left foot shot beyond the dive of Ally Maxwell.

With Gazza now resplendent in new blond dreadlocks, next stop in the league was Fir Park and Captain Courageous Gough – his swollen left eye bruised and battered –

defied the pain of 19 stitches to head home the winner.

September 11 found the Rangers bandwagon in Zurich for the Champions League opener. It didn't so much go off the rails as hurtle down the mountainside.

Rangers didn't look like themselves from the start, clad in an unfamiliar red change strip.

And when the action started they were a pale imitation of the side who had romped home in Russia.

Switzerland's Euro '96 star Kubilay Turkyilmaz dragged them all over the place and they were sent slumping to a 3-0 defeat.

Gough searched long and hard for explanations in the days after that worst possible start and he confessed: "The first game against Grasshopper got us off on a real downer and we just never got off the ground in the Champions League after that.

"But I have to say that I

never saw this season as being built around Europe. It was built around nine-in-a-row.

"I know it's parochial, but that was the feeling from the players and everyone else inside the club.

"We knew it was small-minded in many ways, but it had just come to mean so much."

Three days later, Rangers had the perfect hangover cure, a home clash with Hearts in front of a full house. However, they walked slap-bang into an episode of football farce.

Before the end of an incredible match, referee Gerry Evans and linesman Graeme Alison contrived to make a match without malice resemble a war zone.

Hearts were down to seven men, with Pasquale Bruno, David Weir, Neil Pointon and Paul Ritchie all ordered off and Gough was appealing to the whistler to stop dishing out the cards like a Las Vegas pit boss.

One more red card and the game would have been abandoned, but Rangers had to stay focused on the win and McCoist almost

apologetically rolled in the clincher in a 3-0 cruise.

Rangers, meanwhile, were marching on in the Coca-Cola Cup and Albertz crashed home a classic free-kick in the 4-0 Ibrox quarter-final win over Hibs.

The 32-yard dead-ball belter was later clocked by the Sky TV computer at 78.9mph and Jorg was offi-

cially the hardest shot in Britain!

Smith's side were clicking into gear now and a Gascoigne double at Kilmarnock was overshadowed by a stunning goal from the touch-line by the flu-hit van Vossen.

He was now in such electric form that Durrant insisted his duff twin brother, Archie van Vossen, had been sent over the previous season!

The laughing stopped, though, when the

'I never saw this season as being built around Europe'

GETTING THEIR PRIORITIES RIGHT... *Rangers' search for continental glory (left) played second fiddle to the quest for that coveted ninth successive League Trophy*

Champions League roadshow and French title holders Auxerre came to town.

Thomas Deniaud's double dumped Rangers despite a towering header from Gascoigne. Once more, there was soul-searching to be done just three days before the first Old Firm clash of the season.

And as he checked his tickets for his American adventure, Rangers captain Richard had his usual forth-right views on the way ahead. He insisted: "We've drunk from the well so often in Scotland now and

we have to find another level in Europe.

"I've enjoyed a decade of success but I think it's going to a testing next ten years for the club to progress to the next step up."

N O-ONE should under-esti-mate this intensely-proud man's sense of achievement over nine-in-a-row.

Through seven years of silverware as the club's on-

field leader, he has cher-ished every title win and relished every cup he's brandished in front of a delirious support.

But now that the record they have craved has been matched, Gough insists the fans must broaden their horizons.

He said: "I know I will leave a legacy as captain. I have won more trophies than any other Rangers skipper and that's going to give someone a lot to live up to.

"But I don't think that weight of expectation will

be down to Richard Gough – it will be down to the sheer success of these past years.

"I hope that the pressure is not the same on the players next season.

"People were saying eight titles on the trot would mean nothing unless we made it nine, then others tell me nine means nothing unless we get ten.

"That's pathetic and it should stop. The monkey should be off the club's back now.

"Both Rangers and the fans must look beyond it now the record has been

FIRM FAVOURITE...
Gough celebrates at
Pittodrie and, right, he
powers home a header
for Rangers against
Celtic in October

equalled. What difference will it make if we win another 100 domestic titles. Will we have progressed any?"

I have always found Gough's relationship with the fans difficult to understand.

Sure, there is respect there – they recognise his class. But I firmly believe that they'll never fully appreciate his influence until now when he's gone for good.

He wasn't always a clenched-fists skipper like Terry Butcher or a player like Graham Roberts who openly courted and received the punters' adulation.

Instead, Gough is a man who led by example and, this season more than most, surely showed any doubters the price Rangers have paid when they've been denied his inspiration.

In the wake of that Auxerre defeat, the club needed him to lift the spirits. As always, he was there.

The clash with Celtic was spiced with controversy with Tosh McKinlay red-carded just before the break.

And as Tommy Burns' side tried to recover from that hammer-blow, Rangers rocketed ahead.

Albertz' corner swung out towards the edge of the box and there was the skipper careering in to thunder a header high past Stewart Kerr.

It was the latest in a series of Old Firm strikes. Who could forget his dramatic last-gasp equaliser in 1987 as nine-man Rangers snatched a point in an infamous 2-2 draw?

Naturally, that isn't the one he treasures most. After all, it only brought a point, whereas another goal against Celtic brought a glittering prize.

He smiled: "My header in that 2-0 win was certainly one of my most memorable goals for Rangers. But it would take something special to match scoring the extra-time winner in my first final as skipper to clinch the Skol Cup in 1990."

Old Firm games were to be the proving ground in this historic championship – and, every time, Smith's side strutted off the winners.

That day at Ibrox, they rode their luck in the last minute, looking on in horror as John Hughes' header from a Jackie McNamara cross floated goalwards before smacking back off the bar.

When the ball bounced out, however, the first instinct wasn't to blast it out the park. The first instinct was to kill Celtic stone dead.

Gascoigne sped from defence to feed Albertz and the German raced down the left to swerve a cross into that awful No Man's Land for goalkeepers.

Kerr stayed put and Gazza lunged headlong to bullet home a goal that once again defied those who still claim that, even free of injury, he can't play at full throttle for 90 minutes.

First blood then to Rangers, but they ruined the impetus that gave them with an anaemic display at Easter Road on October 12.

Another Albertz special from a free kick put them in control

But, in a bout of complacency, they were mugged by a penalty from Darren Jackson and a Graeme Donald goal.

The first league defeat of the season had been needlessly conceded and all of a sudden the club were heading towards a crisis centred around controversial Geordie Gascoigne.

As allegations of wife-beating flew at home, Gazza saw red in Amsterdam for lashing out at Ajax defender Winston Bogarde as the Scottish champions slumped to a 4-1 defeat.

The pressure on the shamed England midfielder when he returned for the league showdown with

'I hope the pressure is not the same next season'

Aberdeen on October 22 was intense. But, typically, he responded with a wonder-goal as he curled a stupendous free-kick into the top corner beyond the bemused Nicky Walker.

A mind-blowing Laudrup solo goal made it two, but Brian Irvine and then Billy Dodds at the death turned the game on its head.

Parkhead has proved a happy hunting ground for Rangers in recent seasons and the Coca-Cola Cup Final with Dunfermline proved no exception as Rangers racked up a sizzling 6-1 win.

Erik Bo Andersen continued his remarkable "start-a-game-and-net-a-double" scoring record, the second a thriller as he gunned in a left-foot drive that roared into the roof of the net.

GASCOIGNE then bagged a treble in a 5-0 Ibrox thumping of Motherwell before another Euro KO from Ajax that at least offered a little chink of light at the end of the long, dark tunnel.

Rangers were forced to field a makeshift side, but rookies Greg Shields and Scott Wilson in defence both showed enormous promise for the future as they coped well against the likes of Patrick Kluivert.

But it was still a 1-0 defeat thanks to Arnold Scholten's strike from distance and a sloppy 2-2 draw at Raith sent Rangers into the second Old Firm dust-up of the season in shaky form.

Manager Smith faces constant sniping at his tactics in Europe and the record there, aside from the 1993 glory run, ensures for now that will always be the case.

But domestically, when the chips are down, against Celtic he is the master.

He proved it once more in a bewildering Parkhead match on November 14 with McCoist and van Vossen benched and Bo Andersen in the stand.

The fans questioned why Laudrup was the sole striker, but he revelled in his lone Ranger role and seized on a Brian O'Neil mistake to sweep home the winner in a game that saw both sides squander a host of chances.

Gascoigne missed a penalty for Rangers, van Hooijdonk matched his blunder for Celtic and van Vossen came off the bench to fire over an open goal from six yards!

Laudrup smiled: "We always cringe at Miss of the Week in the columns of the *Rangers News*. Well, that could have been Miss of the

Century. It could have been 7-3 to us never mind 1-0. I know I'll never play in another match like that against Celtic in my life.

"You know, I've played for Milan in a 2-1 win over Inter in the San Siro and it was a spectacular experience but that night at Parkhead was just unbelievable."

It took Rangers into Europe on a mission to retrieve some pride and there was delight for McCoist, who broke his Champions League duck at last with both goals in a 2-1 win over Grasshopper.

Now, just ten days after that Celtic win, Smith's overworked side faced the task of gleaning their first silverware of the season from the Coca-Cola Cup Final with Hearts at Parkhead.

They did it in a 4-3 thriller, but not before their feuding stars had turned the dressing-room into a half-time war zone.

McCoist plundered two superb goals to put his side seemingly on Easy Street but then had a furious row with Gascoigne before Stevie Fulton smacked Hearts back into it.

GOUGH winced: "We were 2-0 up and winning comfortably and then everyone started trying tricks and fancy flicks.

"Gascoigne and McCoist had a head-to-head which continued on the way up the tunnel.

"It was overheating in the dressing-room and there are times when it's like that you'll see the manager just let people have their say.

"It got sorted and there a lot of times when our dressing-room has been like that, simply because it is full of winners."

John Robertson then hauled Hearts level but Gascoigne – bucked up by a half-time double whisky – suddenly put the foot on the gas.

Pasquale Bruno made the fatal mistake of backing off the Geordie and he deftly passed the ball into the net for his first before working a sublime 1-2 with Charlie Miller to sidefoot home another to make it 4-2.

In what seemed like the blink of an eye the man who had caused the club so much torment had won the cup.

David Weir's late goal was only a consolation for the Jambos and Gough admitted: "I remember going out and losing the equaliser and thinking we'd struggle.

"But then Gazza came up with the magic as only he can do to win it for us".

Understandably, Rangers were on a high now and perhaps their best away display of the season earned a 3-0 win at Aberdeen with Laudrup lofting home an exquisite goal to rub in their superiority.

A 2-1 Champions League defeat in Auxerre was meaningless apart from Gough's headed goal on his Euro farewell – once more it was back to the drawing board on that score.

PALLY WITH ALLY... but relations during the nine-in-a-row run-in were sometimes stretched

Traditionally, Christmas brings Rangers the present they want, a dominant lead at the top of the table.

But home wins over Hibs and Dunfermline sandwiched a loss at Tannadice when Gough diverted a cross beyond Goram for an own goal.

Andersen rapped in a hat-trick in a 4-2 win over Kilmarnock before Hearts were outclassed 4-1 at Tynecastle.

RAITH were humbled 4-0 on Boxing Day and, for the third time that season, Celtic were on the agenda – once more they were sent home pointless by the flu-ridden champs.

Virus victim Gough lay in bed in his plush Glasgow mansion watching on television as his side, also hurtfully without Laudrup, won 3-1 thanks to enigmatic Dane Erik Bo.

Albertz had cemented a free-kick beyond the Hoops' wall to put Rangers in front, but Paolo di Canio levelled it. Then Andersen silenced an army of critics within 14 glorious minutes.

His ungainly style earns criticism, his first touch at times derision, but give him a chance in front of goal and his scoring ratio speaks for itself.

He swooped that night with two clinical finishes and later revealed: "The 14 minutes I played actually felt like 90 because of the flu.

"But it was extra-special because my family were there to see it. They thought the roof had come off the stadium after the first and after the second they thought the heavens had opened!"

Andersen hit the target once more in a 2-1 win at Hibs before snatching two as Aberdeen were crushed 4-0 at Ibrox.

Gascoigne then secured a point at Tennents Scottish Cup finalists Kilmarnock before the introduction of the latest striker who will attempt to fill the boots of Super Ally in the years to come, £3.8million Chilean sensation Sebastian Rozental.

Chunky hitman Seb played a bit part as a substitute in a 3-1 win at Motherwell as Albertz grabbed his sixth goal in seven games in a thriller.

Rangers were now eight points clear of Celtic but Rozental was to fall foul of the knee injury curse which has blighted so many Rangers stars after scoring in his next match, the 2-0 Cup win over St Johnstone.

Depressingly, he was out

IN ANOTHER LEAGUE...
Gough hoists aloft another League trophy at Ibrox

'Gazza and McCoist had a head to head in the tunnel'

'I wanted my destiny in my own hands'

WELCOME HOME... Hateley's return to Ibrox for nine-in-a-row certainly proved popular

for the season and Hearts then grabbed a 0-0 Ibrox draw.

Dunfermline, though, were disposed of 3-0 on the back of another screamer from The Hammer as the countdown began to ten make-or-break days in March that would bring two monumental clashes with Celtic.

The satisfaction of a 3-1 home win over Hibs was tempered by frustration after a sloppy display in a 2-2 draw at Aberdeen that featured a bizarre own goal from Andy Goram as he helped Jamie Buchan's cross into Rangers' net.

Then on March 6, in the Scottish Cup last eight, Rangers simply weren't at the races as Malky Mackay and Paolo di Canio sent them tumbling out.

Smith's side, with keeper Goram struggling badly with a host of injuries and Gough troubled by a calf knock, were now looking there for the taking. Six days later,

Dundee United boss Tommy McLean didn't need a second invitation as he masterminded a 2-0 triumph.

With the winning post in sight, Rangers looked fretful and fragile and the pace of Robbie Winters and Swede Kjell Olofsson ripped them to shreds.

Now they were cornered like a fighter on his last legs, backed against the ropes and looking for a way out.

And they were facing the ultimate test against a hungry Celtic side at Parkhead on March 16.

Smith was forced into the recruitment of goalkeeper Andy Dibble, who completed a remarkable transformation as he was rocketed from Manchester City's third team into the Ibrox line-up.

And, at the age of 35, there was also a romantic return to Rangers for Mark Hateley, brought back to Ibrox from QPR.

For Gough, this was THE match, the game that could be the spark to clinch nine-in-a-row.

There was no way he was going to miss it and he

explained: "Injury or no injury, I wanted my destiny in my own hands.

"I'd trained two days before the game and I really should have trained five.

"Yet I knew that, if we lost the game, we'd end up losing the title and, equally, victory would see us win it."

He added: "I knew the stakes and it worked out because, in truth, it was such a very poor game. I was disappointed in Celtic.

"I simply didn't have any last-gasp tackles, last-ditch headers or anything to stretch me."

Smith's patched-up troops went into the game rated underdogs but when it mattered, it was the players in light blue jerseys who had the necessary bottle.

It was an awful match but the outstanding Durrant helped clinch it, latching on to Alan Stubbs' weak back-header and lobbing Stewart Kerr for Laudrup to bundle home.

In an ill-tempered game, Hateley's dream comeback turned into a nightmare when he was red-carded, but Mackay soon joined him. He'd lasted just under an

hour, but it was enough to help swing the pendulum in his favour.

Gough insisted: "Mark's signing was very important.

"We needed someone because, by Ally's own admission, he hadn't played enough to get his usual sharpness.

"Hateley helped us puncture them badly – it seemed to take so much out of them."

It was to be the game that tore the heart out of Tommy Burns' Celtic and eventually cost him his job. In four league games against

Rangers, he'd lost the lot and he paid the ultimate footballing price.

Gough said: "The key to the title was the Grand Slam over Celtic – that's what got us there. I feel that's been the biggest difference between our nine-in-a-row campaign and Celtic's – we've had to face them four times each season.

"But, in the end, they are vastly differing eras and they have both been superb achievements."

Yet, just six days after that dramatic win over the Hoops, Rangers blew it

again, losing 2-1 at home to Kilmarnock as the pressure once more bore down on them.

THE title still beckoned if they could stay on form and a vintage Hateley strike helped to humble Dunfermline 4-0 before Smith moved to the brink of nine-in-a-row in the 6-0 demolition of Raith.

That match marked the return of Gascoigne three

months after suffering an ankle ligament injury in those Amsterdam Sixes.

And there were signs amid a premature Stark's Park title party that the fans were ready to at least give him another chance after all his troubles.

He seemed eager to please, sending an exquisite 40-yard ball to McCoist for a goal especially savoured by the 34-year-old striker who was warming the bench for the eighth game running.

And so to Ibrox on May 5 and the biggest let down any Rangers fan will suffer

BACKING A WINNER...
Jorg Albertz gets a lift
to the party from team-
mate David Robertson
after the final whistle at
Tannadice

'Gough's flight tickets to Kansas were ripped up'

for many years. Nine-in-a-row up for grabs at home in front of a 50,000 full house with the action flashing down from the magnificent new Jumbotron screens in two corners of the stadium.

Gough had announced it would be his Ibrox farewell, declaring his intention to quit for the States the minute the championship was tied up.

It seemed relegation-haunted Motherwell should be cannon fodder, but they didn't read the script as two goals from Owen Coyle rocked Ibrox to its foundations.

Gough's flight tickets to Kansas, a place he feels reminds him of his native Johannesburg, were ripped up.

He was staying for the next instalment on Tayside 48 hours later and led his shattered side on to the team bus as they headed for a hideaway break at St Andrews.

It proved to be a Smith masterstroke. Against Motherwell, his men had been jittery and jaded. Against Dundee United, they were transformed with the restored Charlie Miller a revelation.

From the moment they strode out at Tannadice that night, they looked a side intent on glory despite the absence of crocks Gough and Hateley.

And a journey towards greatness that began with Gary Stevens' goal against Hamilton Accies nine years before ended when Miller whipped in a near-post cross for Laudrup to launch

'There is no better way to leave than with nine-in-a-row behind you'

in for a thrilling header. It was his 20th goal of another sparkling season and the Dane would become only the third man to win a second Player of the Year trophy from the football writers – matching the record of Rangers legends John Greig and Sandy Jardine.

But for Gough, it was bittersweet as he walked around Tannadice at last clutching that League Trophy once more but clad in his club blazer instead of his No.4 jersey.

Yet the skipper-in tears as he accepted the trophy-believes he's right to go out at the top.

He said: "I made my decision early in the season because I didn't want people thinking my choice depended on whether we won the

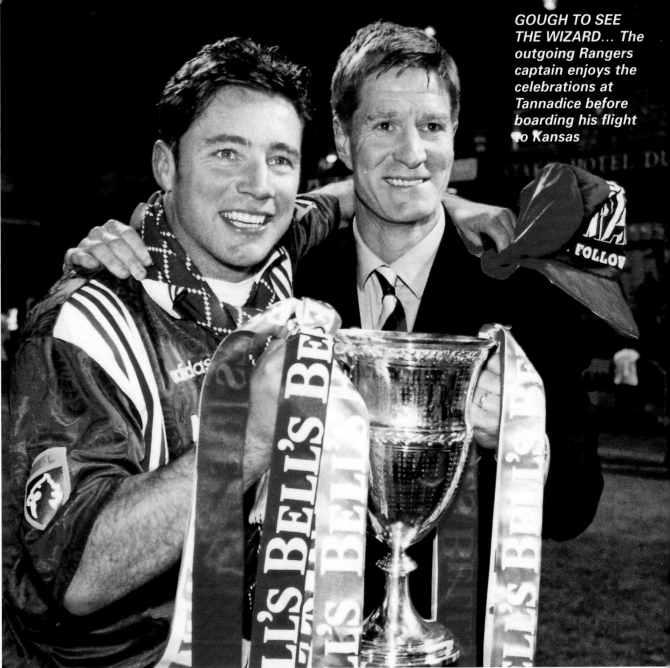

league or not. And I'm not going to America for the money.

"I'm going for the opportunity it gives myself and my family to experience something different.

"Sandy Jardine has also told me I'll get a freshness from leaving now, which he knows from his experience of leaving Rangers for Hearts later on in his career.

"And if I'm going to come back to Britain in some capacity in football then I have always felt it would be better to go away first and come back rejuvenated.

"I'm not retiring, I'm looking forward to new football challenges – or should I say soccer!"

Gough was sometimes reflective and on the fringe of the celebrations as his team-mates indulged in a mimicking of Celtic's huddle with the overjoyed manager flying high into the middle!

BUT as Smith and the captain posed together on the Tannadice turf with the trophy that has become their own property over the last nine years, one overwhelming thought suddenly struck every Rangers fan there.

The man who Walter Smith believes did as much for Rangers as Billy McNeill did for Celtic would have to somehow be replaced.

It will be Smith's toughest task, yet a modest Gough said: "I've never wanted to outstay my welcome or to get to the situation where Walter had to drop me because I wasn't playing too well.

"It's not the same as Terry Butcher, who had a bad knee injury and wasn't quite the same player when he left.

"I've never had a serious injury like that because I've been lucky.

"I simply wanted to leave everyone with good memories – and there is no better way to leave than with nine-in-a-row behind you."

Nine in a row.
No sweat.

Healthy savings every day.

DISCOUNT TOILETRY STORES THROUGHOUT SCOTLAND.

THE UNTOUCHABLES
D.I.Y. TRADE CENTRE
(SCOTLAND) LTD.

Situated in Motherwell, The Untouchables specialise in exclusive wallcoverings from all over Europe including designs from Crowsons, Harlequin and Anna French.

The associated company, Capones in Glasgow, is the largest independent warehouse in Scotland stocking over 300,000 rolls of wallpaper and in excess of 50,000 borders.

Both stores have a computerised paint section with over 3,500 colours to choose from.

The Untouchables are now producing a new range of designs of Rangers wallpaper and accessories, including Broxi Bear for the Kids! **Available from all good wallpaper stores.**

1/7 MOLENDINAR STREET, GLASGOW. TELEPHONE 0141 552 4399

---

131 MERRY STREET, MOTHERWELL. TELEPHONE 01698 264591

THE MEN WHO MADE HISTORY

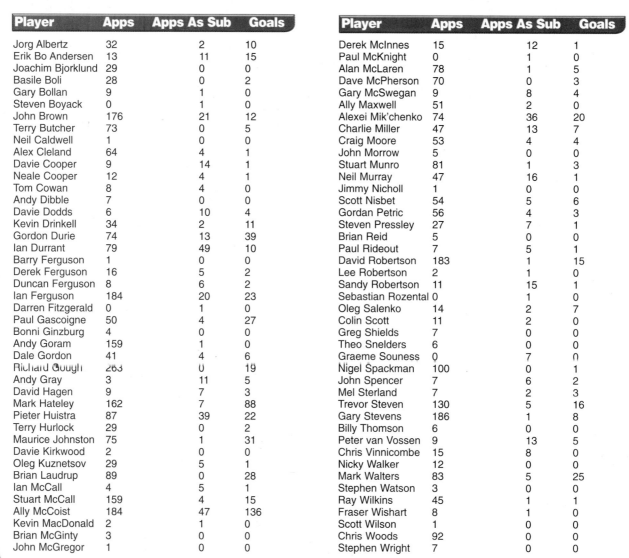

Player	Apps	Apps As Sub	Goals
Jorg Albertz	32	2	10
Erik Bo Andersen	13	11	15
Joachim Bjorklund	29	0	0
Basile Boli	28	0	2
Gary Bollan	9	1	0
Steven Boyack	0	1	0
John Brown	176	21	12
Terry Butcher	73	0	5
Neil Caldwell	1	0	0
Alex Cleland	64	4	1
Davie Cooper	9	14	1
Neale Cooper	12	4	1
Tom Cowan	8	4	0
Andy Dibble	7	0	0
Davie Dodds	6	10	4
Kevin Drinkell	34	2	11
Gordon Durie	74	13	39
Ian Durrant	79	49	10
Barry Ferguson	1	0	0
Derek Ferguson	16	5	2
Duncan Ferguson	8	6	2
Ian Ferguson	184	20	23
Darren Fitzgerald	0	1	0
Paul Gascoigne	50	4	27
Bonni Ginzburg	4	0	0
Andy Goram	159	1	0
Dale Gordon	41	4	6
Richard Gough	263	0	19
Andy Gray	3	11	5
David Hagen	9	7	3
Mark Hateley	162	7	88
Pieter Huistra	87	39	22
Terry Hurlock	29	0	2
Maurice Johnston	75	1	31
Davie Kirkwood	2	0	0
Oleg Kuznetsov	29	5	1
Brian Laudrup	89	0	28
Ian McCall	4	5	1
Stuart McCall	159	4	15
Ally McCoist	184	47	136
Kevin MacDonald	2	1	0
Brian McGinty	3	0	0
John McGregor	1	0	0

Player	Apps	Apps As Sub	Goals
Derek McInnes	15	12	1
Paul McKnight	0	1	0
Alan McLaren	78	1	5
Dave McPherson	70	0	3
Gary McSwegan	9	8	4
Ally Maxwell	51	2	0
Alexei Mik'chenko	74	36	20
Charlie Miller	47	13	7
Craig Moore	53	4	4
John Morrow	5	0	0
Stuart Munro	81	1	3
Neil Murray	47	16	1
Jimmy Nicholl	1	0	0
Scott Nisbet	54	5	6
Gordan Petric	56	4	3
Steven Pressley	27	7	1
Brian Reid	5	0	0
Paul Rideout	7	5	1
David Robertson	183	1	15
Lee Robertson	2	1	0
Sandy Robertson	11	15	1
Sebastian Rozental	0	1	0
Oleg Salenko	14	2	7
Colin Scott	11	2	0
Greg Shields	7	0	0
Theo Snelders	6	0	0
Graeme Souness	0	7	0
Nigel Spackman	100	0	1
John Spencer	7	6	2
Mel Sterland	7	2	3
Trevor Steven	130	5	16
Gary Stevens	186	1	8
Billy Thomson	6	0	0
Peter van Vossen	9	13	5
Chris Vinnicombe	15	8	0
Nicky Walker	12	0	0
Mark Walters	83	5	25
Stephen Watson	3	0	0
Ray Wilkins	45	1	1
Fraser Wishart	8	1	0
Scott Wilson	1	0	0
Chris Woods	92	0	0
Stephen Wright	7	0	0

ONE IN A ROW — Season 1988 - 89

Small figures denote goalscorers

Date	Venue	Opponents	Results	Woods C.	Stevens G.	Munro S.	Gough R.	Wilkins R.	Butcher T.	Drinkell K.	Brown J.	McCoist A.	Durrant I.	Walters M.	Ferguson D.	Cooper D.	Souness G.	Ferguson I.	Nisbet S.	Gray A.	Cooper N.	Walker J.N.	MacDonald K.	McCall I.	McSwegan G.	Nicholl J.	Cowan T.	Sterland M.	Kirkwood D.	Robertson A.
Aug 13	A	Hamilton Accies	2-0	1	2¹	3	4	5	6	7	8	9¹	10	11	12	14														
20	H	Hibernian	0-0	1	2		4	5	6	7	3	9	10	11	8	14	12													
27	H	Celtic	5-1	1	2		4	5¹	6	7²	3	9¹	10	11¹		14	12	8												
Sep 3	A	Motherwell	2-0	1	2		4	5	6	7¹	3		10¹	11			9	8												
17	A	Heart of Midlothian	2-1	1	2		4	5	6	7	3		10¹	11			9	12	8	14¹										
24	H	St. Mirren	2-1	1	2		4	5	6		3		10	11¹			9¹	12	8	7	14									
27	A	Dundee United	1-0	1	2	3	4	5	6			9	10	11				12	8¹	7										
Oct 1	H	Dundee	2-0	1	2	3	4	5	6	7¹	10	9		11¹				12	8	14										
8	A	Aberdeen	1-2	1	2	12	4		6	7	3	9	10	11		14		8			5¹									
12	A	Hibernian	1-0	1	2		4	5	6	7	3	9¹		11		14		8		10										
29	A	St. Mirren	1-1	1	2	3	4	5	6	7		11	9	12				8		14¹	10									
Nov 1	H	Heart of Midlothian	3-0	1	2		4¹	5	6	7	3		11¹					8	9	14¹	10									
5	H	Motherwell	2-1	1	2		4	5	6	7¹	3¹		11	12				8	9	14	10									
12	A	Celtic	1-3	1	2		4	5	6	7	3		11¹	9				8		14	10									
16	H	Hamilton Accies	3-1	1	2	3	4	5	6	7¹		11		14				8¹	12	9¹	10	1								
19	A	Dundee	0-0		2	3	4	5	6	7	10	11						8	9			1								
26	H	Aberdeen	1-0		2		4¹	5	6	7	3	11		9				8			10	1	12							
Dec 3	H	Dundee United	0-1		2		4	5	6	7	3			9				8	14	10	1	11								
10	A	Heart of Midlothian	0-2		2		4	5	6	7	3	11		9				8	14		1	10								
17	H	Hibernian	1-0		2	3	4	5	6	7	9			11	12	8					1		10¹							
31	A	Hamilton Accies	1-0		2	3	4	5	6	7				12¹		8		9	11	1		10	14							
Jan 3	H	Celtic	4-1		2	3	4¹	5	6¹	7	10	11²	9			8			12	1		14								
7	A	Motherwell	1-2		2	3	4	5	6	7¹	10	11	9			8			1	14										
14	A	Aberdeen	2-1		2	3¹	4	5	6	7	10	11	9¹			8			12	1										
21	H	Dundee	3-1		2	3		5	6¹	7	10	14¹	11	9		8¹			12	1					4					
Feb 11	A	Dundee United	1-1		2	3¹	4	5	6	7	10	11	9			8			1											
25	H	St. Mirren	3-1	1	2	3	4	5	6			9¹	10	11	14	8¹			12	7										
Mar 11	H	Hamilton Accies	3-0	1	2		4¹		6	7		9	10	11		8¹										3	5¹			
25	A	Hibernian	1-0	1	2	3	4	12	6	7¹		9	10	11		8											5			
Apr 1	A	Celtic	2-1	1	2	3	4	5	6	7¹	10	9¹		11		14		8									12			
8	H	Motherwell	1-0	1	2	3	4	5	6	7	10	9¹		11	12	8											8			
22	A	St. Mirren	2-0	1	2		4	5	6	7	3	9¹		10	11	14		8¹									12			
29	H	Heart of Midlothian	4-0	1	2	3	4	5	6	7²		9		10	11	14											12	8²		
May 2	H	Dundee United	2-0	1	2	3	4			7¹	6	9¹		11		14	12										10	8	5	
6	A	Dundee	2-1	1	2	3	4				6	9			11			7⁸				14					10	8	5	12
13	H	Aberdeen	0-3	1		3	4		6	7	10	9		11		12		8	14								2			5
TOTAL FULL APPEARANCES				24	35	21	35	30	34	32	29	18	8	30	12	9	30	5	3	11	12	2	2	1	1	3	7	2	1
TOTAL SUB APPEARANCES						1		1					1		1	4	14	6		2		10	3		1		3	1	2	3	
TOTAL GOALS SCORED					1	2	4	1	2	12	1	9	2	8	2		2			6	1	5	1						

FINAL TABLE

	P	W	L	D	F	A	Pts
RANGERS	**36**	**26**	**6**	**4**	**62**	**26**	**56**
Aberdeen	36	18	4	14	51	25	50
Celtic	36	21	11	4	66	44	46
Dundee Utd	36	16	8	12	44	26	44
Hibernian	36	13	14	9	37	36	35
Hearts	36	9	14	13	35	42	31
St Mirren	36	11	18	7	39	55	29
Dundee	36	9	17	10	34	48	28
Motherwell	36	7	16	13	35	44	27
Hamilton Acc	36	6	28	2	19	76	14

TWO IN A ROW — Season 1989 - 90

TRANSFERS

OUT

Player	To	Fee
Andy Gray		Released
Mel Sterland	Leeds	£700,000
Davie Kirkwood	Hearts	£100,000
Avi Cohen	Maccabi	Free
Davie Cooper	Motherwell	£100,000
Nicky Walker	Hearts	£100,000
Kevin Drinkell	Coventry	£900,000
Ray Wilkins	QPR	Free
Ian McCall	Bradford	£125,000

IN

Player	From	Fee
Trevor Steven	Everton	£1,500,000
Mo Johnston	Nantes	£1,500,000
Bonni Ginzburg	Maccabi	£300,000
Davie Dodds	Aberdeen	£200,000
Chris Vinnicombe	Exeter	£300,000
Nigel Spackman	QPR	£500,000

Appearances — Small figures denote goalscorers

Date	Venue	Opponents	Results	Woods C.	Stevens G.	Munro S.	Gough R.	Wilkins R.	Butcher T.	Steven T.	Ferguson I.	McCoist A.	Johnston M.	Walters M.	Ferguson D.	Drinkell K.	Ginzburg B-Z.	Brown J.	Nisbet S.	Cowan T.	Dodds D.	Cooper N.	McCall I.	Spackman N.	Vinnicombe C.	Robertson A.	Souness G.
Aug 12	H	St. Mirren	0-1	1	2	3	4	5	6	7	8	9	10	11	12	14											
19	A	Hibernian	0-2		2	3	4	5	6	7	8	9	10	11		14	1										
26	A	Celtic	1-1		2	3	4	5	6¹	7	8	14	10	9			1		11								
Sep 9	H	Aberdeen	1-0	1	2	3		5	6	7	8	14	10¹	11		9		4	12								
16	H	Dundee	2-2	1	2	3		5	6	7	12	9²	10	11	8				4								
23	A	Dunfermline Ath.	1-1	1	2	3	4	5	6	7	12	9¹	10	11	8												
30	H	Heart of Midlothian	1-0		2	3	4	5	6	7	8	9	10¹	11			1				12	14					
Oct 3	A	Motherwell	0-1		2	3	4	5	6	7		9	10				1				8	11	14				
14	H	Dundee United	2-1	1	2	3	4	5	6	7		9¹	10¹	11							12	8	14				
25	A	St. Mirren	2-0	1	2	3	4	5	6	7	8	9¹	10¹										11				
28	H	Hibernian	3-0	1	2	3	4	5	6	7	8	9²	10¹								14	12	11				
Nov 4	H	Celtic	1-0	1	2	3		5	6	7	8	9	10¹	11				4									
18	A	Dundee	2-0	1	2	3		5	6	7	8	9	10¹	11¹				4	14		12						
22	A	Aberdeen	0-1	1	2	3		5	6	7	8	9	10	11				4									
25	H	Dunfermline Ath.	3-0	1	2	3		5	6¹	7	8	9¹	10¹	11				4									
Dec 2	A	Heart of Midlothian	2-1	1	2	3			6	7¹	8	9	10	11¹				4						5			
9	H	Motherwell	3-0	1	2	3	4		6¹	7	8	9¹	10					11¹						5		14	
16	A	Dundee United	1-1	1	2	3	4		6	7	8	9	10¹					11						5			
23	H	St. Mirren	1-0	1	2	3	4		6	7	8	9	10					11			12¹			5	14		
30	A	Hibernian	0-0	1	2	3	4		6			9	10	7				11	8					5			
Jan 2	A	Celtic	1-0	1	2	3	4		6	7		9	10	8				11						5¹	14		
6	H	Aberdeen	2-0	1	2	3	4		6	7		9¹	10	8¹				11						5	14		
13	H	Dundee	3-0	1	2	3	4		6	7		9¹	10¹	8				11			12¹			5			
27	A	Dunfermline Ath.	1-0	1	2¹	3	4			7		9	10	8				11	6					5			
Feb 3	H	Dundee United	3-1	1	2	3	4			7		9¹	10¹	8¹				11						5	6	14	
10	A	Motherwell	1-1	1	2	3			6	7	4	9	10¹	8				11			12			5			
17	H	Heart of Midlothian	0-0	1	2	3			6	7	4	9	10	8				11						5			
Mar 3	A	Dundee	2-2	1	2	3			6	7	8		10¹					11	4		9¹			5	14		
17	A	St Mirren	0-0	1	2	3	4		6	7	8		10					11	9		12			5			
24	H	Hibernian	0-1	1	2	3	4		6	7	14	9	10	8				11						5			
Apr 1	H	Celtic	3-0	1	2	3	4		6	7	8	9¹	10¹	11¹				14						5			
8	A	Aberdeen	0-0	1	2	3	4		6	7	8	9	10	11				14			12			5			
14	H	Motherwell	2-1	1		3	4		6	7¹		9	10¹	11	14			2			12	8		5			
21	A	Dundee United	1-0	1	2	3	4		6	7¹		9	10	11	8			14						5			
28	H	Dunfermline Ath.	2-0	1	2	3	4		6	7		9¹	10	11				8			12¹			5			14
May 5	A	Heart of Midlothian	1-1	1	2	3¹	4		6			9	10	11				8		7	14			5	12		
TOTAL FULL APPEARANCES				32	35	36	26	15	34	34	21	32	36	27	3	2	4	24	4	1	4	2	2	21	1		1
TOTAL SUB APPEARANCES											3	2			2	2		3	3	2	10	1	2		6	1	1
TOTAL GOALS SCORED					1	1			3	3		14	15	5				1			4			1			

FINAL TABLE

	P	W	L	D	F	A	Pts
RANGERS	**36**	**20**	**5**	**11**	**48**	**19**	**51**
Aberdeen	36	17	9	10	56	33	44
Hearts	36	16	8	12	54	35	44
Dundee Utd	36	11	12	13	36	39	35
Celtic	36	10	12	14	37	37	34
Motherwell	36	11	13	12	43	47	34
Hibernian	36	12	14	10	34	41	34
Dunfermline	36	11	17	8	37	50	30
St Mirren	36	10	16	10	28	48	30
Dundee	36	5	17	14	41	65	24

TRANSFERS

OUT
Derek Ferguson	Hearts	£750,000
Lindsay Hamilton	St Johnstone	Free
Terry Butcher	Coventry	£400,000

IN
Mark Hateley	Monaco	£1,000,000
Pieter Huistra	FC Twente	£250,000
Terry Hurlock	Millwall	£300,000
Oleg Kuznetsov	Dinamo Kiev	£1,200,000
Brian Reid	Morton	£300,000

THREE IN A ROW — Season 1990 - 91

Small figures denote goalscorers

Date	Venue	Opponents	Results	Woods C.	Stevens G.	Brown J.	Gough R.	Spackman N.	Butcher T.	Steven T.	Ferguson I.	Hateley M.	Johnston M.	Walters M.	McCoist A.	Huistra P.	Hurlock T.	Munro S.	Kuznetsov O.	Nisbet S.	Roberston A.	McSwegan G.	Vinicombe C.	Dodds D.	Cowan T.	Spencer J.	Reid B.	Durrant I.
Aug 25	H	Dunfermline Ath.	3-1	1	2	3	4	5	6	7	8	9^1	10^1	11^1	12	14												
Sep 1	A	Hibernian	0-0	1	2	3	4	5	6	7	8	9	10		14		11											
Sep 8	A	Heart of Midlothian	3-1	1	2		4	5	6	7		9	10	14	8^2	11^1	3											
Sep 15	H	Celtic	1-1	1	2	12	4	5	6	7		9	10	14	8	11	3^1											
Sep 22	A	Dundee United	1-2	1	2	12	4	5	6	7		9	10^1	14	8	11	3											
Sep 29	H	Motherwell	1-0	1	2	6^1	4	5		7		12	10	8	9	11		3										
Oct 6	A	Aberdeen	0-0	1	2	6	4	5		7		12	10	11	9		8	3										
Oct 13	H	St Mirren	5-0	1	2		4	5		7		10^1	11^2	9^2	12	8	3	6										
Oct 20	A	St. Johnstone	0-0	1	2		4	5		7	14	10	11	9	12	8	3	6										
Nov 3	H	Hibernian	4-0	1	2		4	5		7^1	12	10^2	11^1	9	14	8	3			6								
Nov 10	H	Dundee United	1-2	1	2	6		5		7		10	11	9^1		8	3			4	12	14						
Nov 17	A	Motherwell	4-2	1	2^2	6		5			9	10^1	11^1	14			8			4	3	7						
Nov 20	A	Dunfermline Ath.	1-0	1	2	6		5			8^1	10		9		7				4	3	11						
Nov 25	A	Celtic	2-1	1	2	6		5			9	10^1	11	14^1	12	7	3			4	8							
Dec 1	H	Heart of Midlothian	4-0	1	2	6		5			9	10^1	11^1	14^1		7^1	3			4	8							
Dec 8	H	St. Johnstone	4-1	1	2^1	6		5		7		9	10^1	11^2	14	12	8	3		4								
Dec 15	A	St. Mirren	3-0	1	2	6	4	5		7		9^1	10^1	11^1	14		8	3										
Dec 22	H	Aberdeen	2-2	1	2	6	4			7		9	10	11	14^2	12	8	3		5								
Dec 29	A	Dundee United	2-1	1	2	6	4	5			9	10^1	11^1	14	12		3			8					7			
Jan 2	H	Celtic	2-0	1	2	6	4	5			9^1	10	7^1		11	8	3			12								
Jan 5	A	Heart of Midlothian	1-0	1	2	6	4	5			9^1	10	7		11	8	3			12								
Jan 12	H	Dunfermline Ath.	2-0	1	2	6	4	5			9	10^1	7		11^1	8				12		3						
Jan 19	A	Hibernian	2-0	1	2		4	5			9	10^1	7	14	11	8				6		3^1			12			
Feb 9	H	St. Mirren	1-0	1	2	6	4	5		7			8	9^1	11					14	3				10			
Feb 16	H	Motherwell	2-0	1	2	6	4	5		7		9^1		11	10^1	14	8			3								
Feb 26	A	St. Johnstone	1-1	1	2	6	4	5		7		9	8	14	10	12^1	11			3								
Mar 2	H	Aberdeen	0-1	1	2	6	4	5		7		9	10	11		4	8			3								
Mar 9	H	Heart of Midlothian	2-1	1	2		4	5		7^1	6	9		11^1	10	12	8			3								
Mar 24	A	Celtic	0-3	1	2		4	5			8		10		9					6	12					7	3	11
Mar 30	A	Dunfermline Ath.	1-0	1	2^1		4	5			8	9	10	11		14	7			3						12	6	
Apr 6	H	Hibernian	0-0	1	2		4	5			9	8		11	7					3					14	6	10	
Apr 13	H	St. Johnstone	3-0	1	2	4		5			8	9		12^1	7					14	3				11^1	6	10^1	
Apr 20	A	St. Mirren	1-0	1	2			5			8	9		12	7		4	14^1		11	3						10	
Apr 24	A	Dundee United	1-0	1	2	6	4	5			8^1	9	10	7		12				11					3			
May 4	A	Motherwell	0-3	1	2	6		5			8	9	10	11	12	7				4	14				3		12	
May 11	H	Aberdeen	2-0	1	2	6		5			8	9^2	10	11	14	7				4					3		12	
TOTAL FULL APPEARANCES				36	36	25	26	35	5	19	10	30	29	26	15	10	29	14	2	15	7	1	10	3	4	3	3	3
TOTAL SUB APPEARANCES						2					1	3			4	11	17			2	8	1	2			1	2	1
TOTAL GOALS SCORED					4	1				2	1	10	11	12	11	4	2			1						1	1

FINAL TABLE

	P	W	L	D	F	A	Pts
RANGERS	**36**	**24**	**5**	**7**	**62**	**23**	**55**
Aberdeen	36	22	5	9	62	27	53
Celtic	36	17	12	7	52	38	41
Dundee Utd	36	17	12	7	41	29	41
Hearts	36	14	15	7	48	55	35
Motherwell	36	12	15	9	51	50	33
St Johnstone	36	11	16	9	41	54	31
Dunfermline	36	8	17	11	38	61	27
Hibernian	36	6	17	13	24	51	25
St Mirren	36	5	22	9	28	59	19

TRANSFERS

OUT

Player	Club	Fee
Stuart Munro	Blackburn	£300,000
Tom Cowan	Sheffield Utd	£350,000
Neale Cooper	Reading	Free
Terry Hurlock	Southampton	£400,000
Mark Walters	Liverpool	£1,125,000
Chris Woods	Sheff Wed	£1,200,000
Trevor Steven	Marseille	£5,500,000
Mo Johnston	Everton	£1,500,000
Dave McKellar		Free

IN

Player	Club	Fee
Andy Goram	Hibs	£1,000,000
Alexei Mik'chenko	Sampdoria	£2,000,000
David Robertson	Aberdeen	£970,000
Stuart McCall	Everton	£1,200,000
Dave McKellar	Kilmarnock	Free
Dale Gordon	Norwich	£1,200,000
Paul Rideout	Notts County	£300,000

Small figures denote goalscorers
† denotes opponent's own goal

Date	Venue	Opponents	Results	Goram A.	Stevens G.	Robertson D.	Gough R.	Spackman N.	Nisbet S.	Steven T.	Ferguson I.	Hateley M.	Johnston M.	Huistra P.	Robertson A.	McCall S.	Spencer J.	Durrant I.	McCoist A.	Mikhailitchenko A.	Kuznetsov O.	Brown J.	Vinnicombe C.	McGregor J.	Morrow J.	McSwegan G.	Gordon D.	Rideout P.	Pressley S.	Robertson L.
Aug 10	H	St. Johnstone	6-0	1	2	3	4	5	6	7	8¹	9³	10²	11	12															
13	H	Motherwell †	2-0	1	2	3	4	5	6	7¹	8	9	10	11																
17	A	Heart of Midlothian	0-1	1	2	3	4	5	6		8	9	10	11		7	12													
24	H	Dunfermline Ath.	4-0	1	2	3	4	5	6		12		9¹		11¹	7	8¹	10	14¹											
31	A	Celtic	2-0	1	2	3	4	5	6		8	9²	10	11		7														
Sept 7	A	Falkirk	2-0	1	2	3	4	5	6¹		8	9		11¹		12	7	10												
14	H	Dundee United	1-1	1	2	3		5	6		8	9		11			12	7¹	10		4									
21	A	St Mirren	2-1	1	2	3	4	5	6¹			9	10	11¹		7	8													
28	H	Aberdeen	0-2	1	2	3		5	6			9	10	14	8	7	12			11		4								
Oct 5	A	Airdrieonians	4-0	1	2	3		5	6¹			10¹	11	12	8			9²	7	4										
8	H	Hibernian	4-2	1	2	3		5	6			10	11¹	7	8	14		9²			4	12								
12	A	St. Johnstone	3-2	1	2	3		5	6¹				8	11	10	9²				4	7	14								
19	H	Heart of Midlothian	2-0	1	2	3	4	5	6		10		8			9¹	11¹				7									
26	H	Falkirk	1-1	1	2	3	4	5	6		12	10	14		8		9	11			7									
29	A	Dundee United	2-3	1	2	3		5	6	7	10	12	11		8		9²	14		4										
Nov 2	H	Celtic	1-1	1	2	3	4	5	6	8	10		11		7		9¹		14											
9	A	Dunfermline Ath.	5-0	1	2	3	4¹	5	6		10¹		11		8		9¹			14					7²					
16	H	Airdrieonians	4-0	1	2	3¹	4	5			10²		11		8		9¹		6						14	7				
19	A	Hibernian	3-0	1	2	3	4	5			10¹		11		8		9²		6							7				
23	H	St. Mirren	0-1	1	2	3	4	5			10		11		8		9		6						14	7				
30	A	Motherwell	2-0	1	2	3	4¹	5			10				8		9	11	6	12						7¹				
Dec 4	A	Aberdeen	3-2	1	2	3	4	5			10²				8		9¹	11	6	12						7				
7	H	St. Johnstone	3-1	1	2	3	4	5			10¹				8	14	9	11¹	6	12¹						7				
14	A	Falkirk	3-1	1	2	3	4	5			10¹				8¹		9¹	11	6							7				
21	H	Dundee United	2-0	1	2	3	4	5			10		14		8		9²	11	6	12						7				
28	H	Dunfermline Ath.	2-1	1	2¹	3	4		5						8	10	9	11	6	12¹						7¹				
Jan 1	A	Celtic	3-1	1	2	3	4	5			10¹		14		8		9¹	11	6	12¹						7				
4	A	Airdrieonians	0-0	1	2	3	4	5					10		8		9	11	6	8						7				
11	H	Hibernian	2-0	1	2	3	4	5							8		9¹	11	6							7¹	10			
18	H	Motherwell	2-0	1	2	3	4	5			12				8		9¹	11¹	6							7	10			
Feb 1	A	Heart of Midlothian	1-0	1	2	3	4	5							8		10¹	11	6						14	7	9			
8	A	St. Mirren	2-1	1	2	3	4	5							8		9¹	11¹	6							7	10			
25	H	Aberdeen	0-0	1	2	3	4	5			8	10		11			14	9	6							7				
29	H	Airdrieonians	5-0	1	2	3	4	5			8	10³		11			14	9	6¹							7	12¹			
Mar 10	H	Hibernian	3-1	1	2	3		5	4		12	10²		11		8		9¹	6							7				
14	A	Dunfermline Ath.	3-1	1	2	3		5	4¹		12	10		11		8		9	7²	6										
21	H	Celtic	0-2	1	2	3		5	4	7	10			12			9	11	14	6										
28	A	St. Johnstone	2-1	1	2	3	4	5			10²			11		7	8	9	14	6								12		
Apr 7	H	Falkirk	4-1	1	2		4	5						11		8		10	9³	14¹	3	6					7	12		
11	A	Dundee United	2-1	1	2	3	4	5						12		8		10	9	11¹		6¹					7	14		
18	H	St. Mirren	4-0	1	2¹		4	5						14¹		8		10	9²	11		6	3				7			
23	A	Motherwell	2-1	1	2	3		5						7	8			10	9	11²	4						6	12		
28	H	Heart of Midlothian	1-1	1		3		5			10			11	14	8		12	9¹		2	6					4			7
May 2	A	Aberdeen	2-0	1	2	3	4				10				8		6	9²	11								7	5		
TOTAL FULL APPEARANCES				44	43	42	33	42	20	2	12	29	10	25	3	35	4	9	37	24	16	18	1	1	3		23	7		1
TOTAL SUB APPEARANCES									4	1	1	7	3	1	4	1		4	1	3	2	7	1			4		4	1	
TOTAL GOALS SCORED					2	1	2		5	1	1	21	5	5		1		34	10	4						5	1		

FINAL TABLE

	P	W	L	D	F	A	Pts
RANGERS	**44**	**33**	**5**	**6**	**101**	**31**	**72**
Hearts	44	27	8	9	60	37	63
Celtic	44	26	8	10	88	42	62
Dundee Utd	44	19	12	13	66	50	51
Hibernian	44	16	11	17	53	45	49
Aberdeen	44	17	13	14	55	42	48
Airdrieonians	44	13	21	10	50	70	36
St Johnstone	44	13	21	10	52	73	36
Falkirk	44	12	21	11	54	73	35
Motherwell	44	10	20	14	43	61	34
St Mirren	44	6	26	12	33	73	24

TRANSFERS

OUT

Paul Rideout	Everton	£500,000
John Spencer	Chelsea	£450,000
Nigel Spackman	Chelsea	£500,000

IN

Ally Maxwell	Motherwell	£300,000
Dave McPherson	Hearts	£1,300,000
Trevor Steven	Marseille	£2,400,000

FIVE IN A ROW — Season 1992 - 93

Small figures denote goalscorers
† denotes opponent's own goal

Date	Venue	Opponents	Results	Goram A.	Nisbet S.	Robertson D.	Gough R.	McPherson D.	Brown J.	Durrant I.	McCall S.	McCoist A.	Hateley M.	Huistra P.	Rideout P.	Kouznetsov O.	Gordon D.	Mikhailitchenko A.	Steven T.	Maxwell A.	Ferguson I.	Spackman N.	Hagen D.	Robertson A.	Stevens G.	McSwegan G.	Pressley S.	Murray N.	Watson S.	Reid B.	Robertson L.
Aug 1	H	St. Johnstone	1-0	1	2	3	4	5	6	7	8	9¹	10	11	12	14															
4	H	Airdrieonians	2-0	1	2	3	4		6	14	8	9	10¹				5	7¹	11												
8	A	Hibernian	0-0	1	2	3	4	5	6	12	8	9	10				11	14	7												
15	A	Dundee	3-4		2	3	4	5	6	12	8	9²	10				7	11		1	14¹										
22	H	Celtic	1-1	1		3	4	5	6	12¹	8	9	10	11			14	7		2											
29	H	Aberdeen	3-1	1		3	4	5	6	7¹		9¹		11			10¹			8	2										
Sept 2	A	Motherwell	4-1	1		3	4	5	6¹	7		9³		11			10			8	2										
12	A	Partick Thistle	4-1	1		3	4¹	5¹	6	10	2¹	9	12¹	7			11			8											
19	H	Heart of Midlothian	2-0	1		3	4	5	6	10	2¹	9¹						7		8	14										
26	A	Dundee United	4-0	1	5	3			6		2	9¹	10	11²			4		7¹	8		14									
Oct 3	H	Falkirk	4-0	1	2	3		5	6	12	7	9⁴	10	11			4			8											
7	A	St. Johnstone	5-1	1	2	3		5		6	4	9²	10²	11				14	7	8¹											
17	H	Hibernian	1-0	1		3	4		6	9	12	14¹	10	11	2		5	7	8												
31	H	Motherwell	4-2	1		3		5	6¹		7	9³		11	2	4	10			8		12									
Nov 7	A	Celtic	1-0	1		3	4	5	6	11¹	2	9	10	12			7	14		8											
11	H	Dundee	3-1	1		3		5	6	4	7	9²	10¹	11			14			8		2									
21	A	Heart of Midlothian	1-1	1		3		5	6	12		9¹	10	11			4		7	8		2									
28	H	Partick Thistle	3-0	1		3		5¹	6		10			11			4		7¹	8		2	9¹								
Dec 1	A	Airdrieonians	1-1	1		3			6¹	4		10				12	11	7	8		2	9	5								
12	A	Falkirk	2-1	1		3		5	6	4	8	9¹	10¹				7	11			2										
19	H	St. Johnstone	2-0	1		3¹	4¹	5		6	8	9	10	11				7			2										
26	A	Dundee	3-1	1		3	4	5		11	6	9¹	10²				14	7			2										
Jan 2	H	Celtic	1-0	1		3	4	5	6	11	2		10				9	14	7¹	8											
5	H	Dundee United	3-2	1		3	4	5	6		2¹	9¹	10¹	12				11	7	8											
30	A	Hibernian	4-3	1		3		5	6	12	8	9¹	10²	14			4	11	7¹			2									
Feb 2	A	Aberdeen	1-0	1		3		5	6		8	9	10¹				4	11	7			2									
9	H	Falkirk	5-0	1		3¹	4		6		8	9	10²	11¹	5			7¹				2									
13	H	Airdrieonians	2-2	1		3	4		6			9²	10	11	5	14	8	7			12	2									
20	A	Dundee United	0-0	1		3	4	5			7	9	10	11				8			2		6								
23	A	Motherwell	4-0	1		3	4	5	6		2	9¹	10²	11			12¹	7	8				14								
27	H	Heart of Midlothian	2-1	1	2	3¹		5	6		4	9¹	10	11			7	12	8				14								
Mar 10	A	St. Johnstone	1-1		2	3		5	6	12	8	9¹	10					11	7	1			4								
13	H	Hibernian	3-0			3		5	6	8	2	9¹	10¹			12			1			11¹		7	4						
20	A	Celtic	1-2	1	2	3		5	6	11	9	12	10¹				14	7			8			4							
27	H	Dundee	3-0			3	4	5	6		2¹	9¹	10	11			14	7	1	8¹			12								
30	H	Aberdeen	2-0			3	4	5	6		2	9¹	10	11			14	7	1	8¹			12								
Apr 10	H	Motherwell	1-0				4	5	6¹	14	2	9	10	11				7	1	8			3								
14	A	Heart of Midlothian	3-2				6	12	2¹		10²	11					7	1	8			9	5	4	3						
17	A	Partick Thistle	3-1				6		2		10			7			1	8	11¹			9²	5	4	3						
May 1	A	Airdrieonians	1-0	1		3	4	5	6		2	10	11					8			9¹	7									
4	A	Partick Thistle	0-3				4		6	8		10	11	5	7	14	1				9		2	3							
8	H	Dundee United	1-0	1		3	4	5	6	10			11†	2		14		8		7	9	12									
12	A	Aberdeen	0-1				5	6	12				3	7	11	1	8	10		14	2				4	9					
15	A	Falkirk	2-1			3			4	8		10¹			7	11¹	1	12		9	6	2		5							

TOTAL FULL APPEARANCES				34	10	39	25	34	39	19	35	32	36	27		8	18	16	24	10	29	2	5		9	8	8	11	3	2	1
TOTAL SUB APPEARANCES										11	1	2	1	3	1	1	1	4	13		1		3	2		1		4		5	
TOTAL GOALS SCORED						3	2	2	4	3	5	34	21	4			1	3	5		4				4		1			

FINAL TABLE

	P	W	L	D	F	A	Pts
RANGERS	**44**	**33**	**4**	**7**	**97**	**35**	**73**
Aberdeen	44	27	7	10	87	36	64
Celtic	44	24	8	12	68	41	60
Dundee Utd	44	19	16	9	56	49	47
Hearts	44	15	15	14	46	51	44
St Johnstone	44	10	14	20	52	66	40
Hibernian	44	12	19	13	54	64	37
Partick Thistle	44	12	20	12	50	71	36
Motherwell	44	11	20	13	46	62	35
Dundee	44	11	21	12	48	68	34
Falkirk	44	11	26	7	60	86	29
Airdrieonians	44	6	21	17	35	70	29

TRANSFERS

OUT

Gary McSwegan	Notts County	£450,000
Dale Gordon	West Ham	£800,000
Sandy Robertson	Coventry	£250,000

IN

Duncan Ferguson	Dundee Utd	£4,000,000
Fraser Wishart	Free Agent	
Gordon Durie	Tottenham	£1,200,000

SIX IN A ROW — Season 1993 - 94

Small figures denote goalscorers
† denotes opponent's own goal

Date	Venue	Opponents	Results	Maxwell A.	McCall S.	Wishart F.	Gough R.	Pressley S.	Brown J.	Murray N.	Ferguson I.	Hateley M.	Hagen D.	Mikhailitchenko A.	Durrant I.	Huistra P.	Steven T.	Vinnicombe C.	McPherson D.	Ferguson D.	Stevens G.	Robertson D.	Kuznetsov O.	Morrow J.	Miller C.	McCoist A.	Scott C.	Durie G.	Goram A.	Moore C.
Aug 7	H	Heart of Midlothian	2-1	1	2	3	4	5	6	7	8	9¹	10¹	11	12	14														
14	A	St. Johnstone	2-1	1		3	4¹	5	6	2	8¹		9	12	10	11	7	14												
21	A	Celtic	0-0	1		3	4	2		6	8	10	14		12	11	7		5	9										
28	H	Kilmarnock	1-2	1			4	5¹		6	8	10		11	12		7			9	2	3								
Sep 4	A	Dundee	1-1	1			4	5			8	10¹			12	11	7			9	2	3	6							
11	H	Partick Thistle	1-1	1			4				8	10¹			12		7	6	5	9	2	3		11						
18	A	Aberdeen	0-2	1	4				6		8	10				11	7		5	12	2	3			9					
25	H	Hibernian	2-1	1		6	4			14	8	10¹	9	11			7¹		5		2	3								
Oct 2	A	Raith Rovers	1-1	1			4	5		3	8	10			6	11	7			2						9	15			
6	H	Motherwell	1-2				4	5		3	8¹	10	9	14	6	12	7			2				11			1			
9	A	Dundee United	3-1	1	6		4	12			8	10¹			7	9	11²		5		2	3				14				
16	H	St. Johnstone	2-0	1			4				8	10¹			6	12	11¹	7		5	2	3				9				
30	H	Celtic	1-2	1	6		4	14			8	10			12	11	7			5	2	3				9¹				
Nov 3	A	Heart of Midlothian	2-2	1	2		4	14	6		8	10²			7		11			5		3				9				
6	A	Kilmarnock	2-0	1	2		4	14	6		8¹	10			7	11	12¹			5		3				9				
10	H	Dundee	3-1	1	4					6	8¹	10			11	7	14			5	2	3				9²				
13	H	Raith Rovers	2-2	1	5		4			6	8	10²			7	9	11				2	3			14					
20	A	Hibernian	1-0	1	7		4¹		6	2	8	10			11	9				5		3								
27	A	Partick Thistle	1-1	1	2		4		6		8	10			11	9	14¹			5	12	3						7		
Dec 1	H	Aberdeen	2-0	1	2		4	14	6	11	8	10²			12		7			5		3						9		
4	A	Motherwell	2-0	1	4			6			11	8	10		12		7			5	2	3						9²		
11	H	Dundee United	0-3	1	6		4	14			11	8	10		12		7			5	2	3						9		
18	H	St. Johnstone	4-0	1	4			5			8	10²			11		7¹	3		2	6							9¹		
27	H	Heart of Midlothian	2-2	1	4			5	6	3		10²			11		12	7	14	2	8							9		
Jan 1	A	Celtic	4-2	1	8		4	5	6	3		10¹		11²		12	7			2		14¹						9		
8	H	Kilmarnock	3-0	1	8		4		6	5		10²		11		12¹	7			2	3							9		
15	H	Dundee	1-1	1	8			5	6	4		10		11		12	7			2	3	14						9¹		
22	A	Aberdeen	0-0	1	8		4		6	5		10		11		12	7			2	3							9		
Feb 5	H	Partick Thistle	5-1	1	8¹		4		6	5		10		11¹			7¹			2	3							9²		
12	H	Hibernian	2-0		5		4		6		8	10		11			7¹			2	3					14		9¹	1	
26	A	Raith Rovers	2-1		4				6		8¹	10		14			7		5	2	3					9		11¹	1	
Mar 5	H	Motherwell	2-1		5		4		6		8	10¹		11			7		12	2	3					14		9¹	1	
19	H	St. Johnstone	4-0		2¹		4		6		8	10¹					7		5¹		3					9		11¹	1	
26	A	Heart of Midlothian	2-1		3		4		6		8	10¹		12			7		5		2					9¹		11	1	
29	A	Partick Thistle	2-1		3		4¹		6		8	10		11			7		5	14	2					9¹		12	1	
Apr 2	H	Aberdeen	1-1		7¹		4		6	3	8	10		12					5		2					9		11	1	
5	A	Dundee United	0-0	15	7		4	6		3		12		11	8				5	10								9	1	2
16	H	Raith Rovers	4-0	1	2		4		6		8	12		14¹	7				5	10¹	3¹					9¹		11		
23	H	Dundee United	2-1	1	2		4		6		8	10					7		5		3					9		11²		
26	A	Motherwell	1-2	1	2		4	6			8			12			7		5	10	3					9¹		11		
30	H	Celtic	1-1		2		4	6			8	10		12¹			7		5	14	3					9	1	11		
May 3	A	Hibernian	0-1		2		4	6		14	8	10		11	9		7		5		3					12	1			
7	A	Kilmarnock	0-1			2	4			5		10	12	11	7	14					3	6		8	9	1				
14	H	Dundee	0-0		6		4				8	10		12		11	7		5		2	3				14	1	9		

				Max	McC	Wis	Gou	Pre	Bro	Mur	FeI	Hat	Hag	Mik	Dur	Hui	Ste	Vin	McP	FeD	StG	Rob	Kuz	Mor	Mil	McCo	Sco	Dur	Gor	Moo
TOTAL FULL APPEARANCES				31	34	5	37	17	24	20	35	40	4	24	14	10	32	4	27	7	28	32	4	2	2	16	5	23	8	1
TOTAL SUB APPEARANCES				1				6		2		2	2	10	9	11		2	2	1	3	1		2	1	1	5	1	1	
TOTAL GOALS SCORED					3		3	1			5	22	1	5		6	4			1			1	1		7		12		

FINAL TABLE

	P	W	L	D	F	A	Pts
RANGERS	**44**	**22**	**8**	**14**	**74**	**41**	**58**
Aberdeen	44	17	6	21	58	36	55
Motherwell	44	20	10	14	58	43	54
Celtic	44	15	9	20	51	38	50
Hibernian	44	16	13	15	53	48	47
Dundee Utd	44	11	13	20	47	48	42
Hearts	44	11	13	20	37	43	42
Kilmarnock	44	12	16	16	36	45	40
Partick Thistle	44	12	16	16	46	57	40
St Johnstone	44	10	14	20	35	47	40
Raith Rovers	44	6	19	19	46	80	31
Dundee	44	8	23	13	42	57	29

TRANSFERS

OUT

Chris Vinnicombe	Burnley	£200,000
Oleg Kuznetsov	Maccabi Haifa	£400,000
Gary Stevens	Tranmere	£350,000
Steven Pressley	Coventry	£600,000
Dave McPherson	Hearts	Swap for Alan McLaren
David Hagen	Hearts	£250,000
Duncan Ferguson	Everton	£4,200,000
Pieter Huistra	Sanfrecce	£500,000
Fraser Wishart	Hearts	Free

IN

Brian Laudrup	Fiorentina	£2,500,000
Basile Boli	Marseille	£2,700,000
Billy Thomson	Motherwell	£25,000
Alan McLaren	Hearts	Swap for McPherson
Alex Cleland	Dundee Utd	£500,000
Gary Bollan	Dundee Utd	£250,000

SEVEN IN A ROW — Season 1994 - 95

Small figures denote goalscorers

† denotes opponent's own goal

Date	Venue	Opponents	Results	Goram A.	Murray N.	Robertson D.	Gough R.	Boli B.	McPherson D.	Durrant I.	McCall S.	McCoist A.	Hateley M.	Laudrup B.	Ferguson D.	Brown J.	Moore C.	Ferguson I.	Pressley S.	Durie G.	Mikhailitchenko A.	Miller C.	Huistra P.	Hagen D.	Wishart F.	McLaren A.	Scott C.	McGinty B.	Maxwell A.	Steven T.	Bollan G.	Cleland A.	Thomson W.	Robertson L.	Caldwell N.	McKnight P.
Aug 13	H	Motherwell	2-1	1	2	3	4	5	6	7	8	9	10¹	11	14¹																					
20	A	Partick Thistle	†2-0	1			4	5	6		2		10¹	11	9	3	7	8																		
27	H	Celtic	0-2	1			4	5	6	7	2		10	11	12			8	3	9																
Sep 11	H	Heart of Midlothian	3-0	1	7	3	4		5		9	2	10²	11	14		6	8			12¹															
17	A	Falkirk	2-0	1		3	4	5¹		7	2		10	11¹			6	8			9															
24	A	Aberdeen	2-2	1	7	3	4	6	5	12	8		10¹	11			2¹				9															
Oct 1	H	Dundee United	2-0	1	12	3	4	6	5	7	14	10¹	11¹				2					8	9													
8	A	Hibernian	1-2	1	12	3	4	6¹	5	7	14	10	11				2					9	8													
15	H	Kilmarnock	2-0	1	7	3¹		5		4		10	11				2	6				9¹	8													
22	A	Motherwell	†1-2	1	7	3		6	5	4		10	11				2					9	8	14												
30	A	Celtic	3-1	1	8	3		6		4		14	10³	11¹				9	7	12	2	5														
Nov 5	H	Partick Thistle	3-0	1	8	3		6		12	4		10	11¹				9¹	7		2	5														
9	A	Heart of Midlothian	1-1	1	8	3		6		9	4	14	10¹	11	2				7			5														
19	H	Falkirk	1-1	1		3		6		12	4	9	10¹	11	2		14	8	7			5														
25	H	Aberdeen	1-0	1		3		6			4	9¹	10	11			14	8	7		2	5														
Dec 4	A	Dundee United	3-0	1		3	4	6		12	2	9		11¹			10	8	7¹			5														
10	A	Kilmarnock	2-1	1	6	3	4			10	2			11¹			14	9	8	7		5¹														
26	H	Hibernian	2-0			3	4¹	6			2		10¹	11	12			9	8	7		5	1													
31	A	Motherwell	3-1			3	4	6			2			11¹		10	12	9	8	7		5	1													
Jan 4	H	Celtic	1-1			3	4	6			14	2		11	12		8¹	9	10	7		5	1													
7	A	Partick Thistle	1-1	1	11	3¹					9	4			6	2	8			7		5	13	10												
14	A	Falkirk	3-2	10	3					11	4¹				6	2	8			9	7³	14	5			1	12									
21	H	Heart of Midlothian	1-0	10		4	6			12	2			11	3	14	8			9¹		5				1	7									
Feb 4	H	Dundee United	1-1			3¹	4	5			6	14	10	11	12	2				9		8				1	7									
12	A	Aberdeen	0-2			3	4	5		12	8		10	11		2				14		9				1		6	7							
25	H	Kilmarnock	3-0			3	4	6		14¹	2			11²	12					10¹		9				5		1	7		8					
Mar 4	A	Hibernian	1-1	8		4	6			12	10				11	2	14			9¹						5		1	7	3						
11	H	Falkirk	2-2			4	6			7	2			11¹	10¹		8			9	14					5		1		3						
18	A	Heart of Midlothian	1-2	14		4	6			12	10			11¹			8			9						5		1	7	3	2					
Apr 1	A	Dundee United	2-0			4	6			10	7			11	3					9¹	12	8				5					14	2	1			
8	H	Aberdeen	3-2	12¹		4	6			9¹			10¹	11	3					14	8					5			7		2	1				
16	H	Hibernian	3-1	12		4				6¹			10	11	3			2	8	9¹	14¹	8				5			1	3	7	14				
20	A	Kilmarnock	1-0	6		4				9			10	11			2	8		10¹		3				5			7	2	1					
29	H	Motherwell	0-2			4	6			9			10	11			8			3						5			7	2	1					
May 7	A	Celtic	0-3	14			4			9			10	11	6	2	8			12						5			13	7	3	1				
13	H	Partick Thistle	1-1	13						9			10	11		4¹			8	6						5			1	7	3				2	14
TOTAL FULL APPEARANCES				18	14	23	25	28	9	16	30	4	23	33	1	10	19	13	2	16	4	21	15		3	24	3	1	10	10	5	10	5		1	
TOTAL SUB APPEARANCES				1	6					10		5				3	3	2			4	5		2	1		1			1	1	1			1		1
TOTAL GOALS SCORED				1		3	1	2		4	2	1	13	10	1		1	2		6	2	3	3						2							

FINAL TABLE

	P	W	L	D	F	A	Pts
RANGERS	**36**	**20**	**7**	**9**	**60**	**35**	**69**
Motherwell	36	14	10	12	50	50	54
Hibernian	36	12	7	17	49	37	53
Celtic	36	11	7	18	39	33	51
Falkirk	36	12	12	12	48	47	48
Hearts	36	12	17	7	44	51	43
Kilmarnock	36	11	15	10	40	48	43
Partick Th	36	10	13	13	40	50	43
Aberdeen	36	10	15	11	43	46	41
Dundee Utd	36	9	18	9	40	56	36

TRANSFERS

OUT
Ally Maxwell	Dundee Utd	£250,000
Mark Hateley	QPR	£1,000,000
Brian Reid	Morton	£200,000
Oleg Salenko	Istanbulspor	Swap V Vossen

IN
Stephen Wright	Aberdeen	£1,500,000
Paul Gascoigne	Lazio	£4,300,000
Gordan Petric	Dundee Utd	£1,500,000
Oleg Salenko	Valencia	£2,500,000
Derek McInnes	Morton	£350,000
Peter Van Vossen	Istanbulspor	Swap for Salenko
Erik Bo Andersen	Aalborg	£1,500,000

EIGHT IN A ROW — Season 1995 - 96

Small figures denote goalscorers
† denotes opponent's own goal

Player columns (left to right): Goram A., Wright S., Robertson D., Gough R., McLaren A., Petric G., Steven T., Miller C., McCoist A., McCall S., Durie G., Durrant I., Salenko O., Gascoigne P., Laudrup B., Moore C., Murray N., Mikhailitchenko A., Cleland A., Ferguson I., Brown J., Scott C., Bollan G., Thomson W., McGinty B., McInnes D., Van Vossen P., Andersen E.B., Snelders T., Shields G.

Date	Venue	Opponents	Results	Gor	Wri	Rob	Gou	McL	Pet	Ste	Mil	McC(A)	McC(S)	Dur(G)	Dur(I)	Sal	Gas	Lau	Moo	Mur	Mik	Cle	Fer	Bro	Sco	Bol	Tho	McG	McI	VV	And	Sne	Shi
Aug 26	H	Kilmarnock	1-0	1	2	3	4	5	6	7	8	9	10¹	11	12		14																
Sep 9	H	Raith Rovers	4-0	1	2	3¹	4	5	6		7¹	9²			12		10	8	11														
16	A	Falkirk	2-0	1		3¹	4	5	6		10	14	8		9¹		12		2	7	11	15											
23	H	Hibernian	0-1	1	2		4	5	6		7	9	14		10	8	11		16		3												
30	A	Celtic	2-0	1	2		4	5	6		12	9	7		10	8¹					3¹	11											
Oct 3	H	Motherwell	2-1	1			4	5	6		9¹	14	7	12	8¹		2	16	11	3	10												
7	A	Aberdeen	1-0	1	2	3	4	5	6		10	11	8	9		14¹	16		7														
14	A	Partick Thistle	4-0	1	2	3	4¹	5	6		14	10	9³	8		16		11	7		12												
21	A	Heart of Midlothian	4-1	1		3	4	5	6			10¹	12	9²	8¹		2		11	7		16											
28	A	Raith Rovers	2-2	1		4¹	5	6¹	16	9		11		10	8		2	7	14	3													
Nov 4	H	Falkirk	2-0			4	5	6	12	9²	10	11	7				2	8				1	3										
8	A	Kilmarnock	2-0			4	5¹	6	9			7	10¹	8			12	2	11	16	1	3											
11	H	Aberdeen	1-1			4	5	6	14	10		12	9¹	8			11	2	7	16		3	1										
19	H	Celtic	†3-3	1		3	4	5	6		12	14¹	10			9	8	11¹			2	7											
25	A	Hibernian	†4-1	1		4	5	6		7¹	9¹		14	12	10	8			2			3		11									
Dec 2	A	Heart of Midlothian	2-0	1		3	4	5	6	10	9¹	12	14			8¹	11		2					7									
9	H	Partick Thistle	1-0	1		3	4	5	6	7	9	10¹	12			11	2								8								
19	A	Motherwell	0-0	1		3	4	5	6	9		10				11	7		8						2								
26	H	Kilmarnock	3-0	1		3	4	5	6	7		10¹	12	9¹	8¹	11			2						14								
30	H	Hibernian	7-0	1		3	4	5	6	7¹		10⁴		9	8¹	11			2														
Jan 3	A	Celtic	0-0	1		3	4	5	6	7		10		9	8	11			16			2											
6	A	Falkirk	4-0	1		3¹	4	5	6		9²	10¹	16	8			7		2					11									
13	H	Raith Rovers	4-0	1		3	4	5	6		9¹	10²		8	11		12		2¹					7									
20	H	Heart of Midlothian	0-3	1		3	4	5	6	7		10	9			11		12	8	2							14						
Feb 3	A	Partick Thistle	2-1	1		3		5	6	9		10				8²	11		16	2		4				7							
10	H	Motherwell	3-2	1		3		5¹	6	7	14¹	10				8	11	4				2¹				9							
25	A	Aberdeen	1-0	1		3		5	4	7		10				8¹	11	2	14	9	6						12						
Mar 3	A	Hibernian	†2-0	1		3	4	5	6	12	16	10				8	11¹	2				14								7	9		
17	H	Celtic	1-1	1			5¹	4		7	9	10	14			8	11	2				3		6									
23	H	Falkirk	3-2				5	4	2		9	10	12			8¹	11	16	3			6	1							7²			
30	A	Raith Rovers	4-2				5	2			9³	10	4¹			8	11		3	12	6								14	7	1		
Apr 10	A	Heart of Midlothian	0-2	1		3	4	5	6	7		9	10	12		8	11		2	16	14												
13	H	Partick Thistle	5-0	1		3	4¹	5		16		10¹	7			8	11		6												9³		
20	H	Motherwell	3-1	1		3	4	5		2		10¹	7			8¹	11		6												9¹		
28	H	Aberdeen	3-1	1		3	4	5	16	2		14	10	7	12	8³	11		6												9		
May 4	A	Kilmarnock	3-0			3		5		7	16	9¹	4	10²	6		8													11	14	1	2

				Gor	Wri	Rob	Gou	McL	Pet	Ste	Mil	McC(A)	McC(S)	Dur(G)	Dur(I)	Sal	Gas	Lau	Moo	Mur	Mik	Cle	Fer	Bro	Sco	Bol	Tho	McG	McI	VV	And	Sne	Shi
TOTAL FULL APPEARANCES				30	6	25	29	36	32	5	17	18	19	21	6	14	27	22	9	2	6	21	16	8	6	3	4	1	2	5	3	6	2
TOTAL SUB APPEARANCES										1		1	6	7	2	6		2	9	2	1			2	3	5		4	2	6		1	4
TOTAL GOALS SCORED						3	3	3	1		3	16	3	3	17	7	14	2	2			1								6		

FINAL TABLE

	P	W	L	D	F	A	Pts
RANGERS	**36**	**27**	**3**	**6**	**85**	**25**	**87**
Celtic	36	24	1	11	74	25	83
Aberdeen	36	16	13	7	52	42	55
Hearts	36	16	13	7	55	53	55
Hibernian	36	11	15	10	43	57	43
Raith Rovers	36	12	17	7	41	57	43
Kilmarnock	36	11	17	8	39	54	41
Motherwell	36	9	15	12	28	39	39
Partick Th	36	8	22	6	29	62	30
Falkirk	36	6	24	6	31	60	24

TRANSFERS

OUT

Lee Robertson		FREE
Alexei Mikhailichenko		FREE
Colin Scott		FREE
Billy Thomson	Dundee	FREE

TOTAL INCOME £27,450,000

IN

Jorg Albertz	Hamburg	£4,000,000
Joachim Bjorklund	Vicenza	£2,700,000
Sebastian Rozental	U Cattolica	£3,500,000
Mark Hateley	QPR	£400,000
Tony Vidmar	NAC Breda	FREE
Jonas Thern	AS Roma	FREE

TOTAL SPENDING £59,790,000

NINE IN A ROW — Season 1996 - 97

Small figures denote goalscorers

¹ denotes opponent's own goal

Date	Venue	Opponents	Results	Goram A.	Cleland.	Robertson D.	Gough R.	McLaren A.	Bjorklund	I. Ferguson	Gascoigne	McCoist	Albertz	Laudrup	Durrant I.	van Vossen	Moore	Petric	Durie.	McInnes.	McCall.	Miller.	Andersen	Shields	Steven.	Snelders	Dibble.	Hateley	Wilson	Rozental	Wright.	Boyack	Fitzgerald	B.Ferguson
Aug 10	H	Raith Rovers	1-0	1			4	6				9	3	11	12	14		5	7	8	10				2¹									
17	A	Dunfermline	5-2	1	2		4	6			14	9³	3	11	12	7²		5			10	8												
24	H	Dundee United	1-0	1	2		4	6		8¹		9	3	11				5	12	14	10	7												
Sept 7	A	Motherwell	1-0	1	2		4¹	6			8	14	3	11				5	7	9	10	12												
14	H	Hearts	3-0	1	2		4	6		8¹	14¹		3	11	12			5	10¹	9	7													
21	A	Kilmarnock	4-1	1	9		4	6	12	8²			3	11		16²		2	5	7	14	10												
28	H	Celtic	2-0	1	7		4¹	6	14	8¹			3	11		9		2	5		12	10												
Oct 12	A	Hibernian	1-2	1	7		4	6			10	8	3¹	11		9		2	5		12		14								16			
19	H	Aberdeen	2-2		10		4	6	12		8¹		3	11¹	14		7	5					9	2	1									
26	H	Motherwell	5-0			3	4	6			8³	14	10	11²	12			2	5	7			9		1									
Nov 2	A	Raith Rovers	2-2		2	3	4	6			8	9¹	10		7	11¹		5		14			12		1									
14	A	Celtic	1-0	1	2	3	4	6			8	14	10	11¹	12	7		5					9											
Dec 1	A	Aberdeen	3-0	1		3¹	4	6	14		8	9	10	11¹				7	5				12¹	2										
7	H	Hibernian	4-3	1		3	4				10¹	8	9²		11¹			6	12	7			2	14				5						
10	A	Dundee United	0-1	1	2	3	4				10	8	9	11				6	5	7			12					14						
14	H	Dunfermline	3-1	1	2	3	4¹				10	8	9¹		12	11	14	6	5						16¹			7						
17	H	Kilmarnock	4-2	1	2	3¹	4	5	6			8	14	10	11			12							9³			7						
21	A	Hearts	4-1	1	2	3¹	4	5	6			8¹	14	10¹	11¹			12							9			7						
26	H	Raith Rovers	4-0	1	2	3	4¹	5	6			8¹	9¹	10¹	11			12							7	14								
Jan 2	H	Celtic	3-1	1	2	3		5	6	11		8	9	10¹	14		7	4					12	16²										
4	A	Hibernian	2-1		2	3					8		14	10¹	11			6	5	7			12	9¹	4	1								
12	H	Aberdeen	4-0	1	2	3	4	5	6			8	14	10¹	11¹			12		7				9²										
15	A	Kilmarnock	1-1	1	2		4	12	6	7	8¹	9	10	11				3	5	14														
18	A	Motherwell	3-1	1	2	3	4	5		7	8¹	14	10	11					6	12				9¹					16					
Feb 1	H	Hearts	0-0	1	2	3	4	5	6		10	9		11¹			14	12	7	8														
8	A	Dunfermline	3-0	1	2	3	4	5	6			8	14	10¹	11¹			9	12	7¹														
23	H	Hibernian	3-1	1	2	3	4¹	5	6			8	14	10¹	11¹			9	12						7									
Mar 1	A	Aberdeen	2-2	1	2	3		5	6			8	14	10	11¹		7¹	4	9				12											
12	H	Dundee United	0-2	1	2			5	6			8	14	10	11			3	4	7			9	12										
16	A	Celtic	1-0		2		4	5	6			8	14	3	11¹			9	7				12								1	10		
22	H	Kilmarnock	1-2		2			5	6			14	10	11		9		4	12	7¹	8		3								1		16	
Apr 5	H	Dunfermline	4-0		2	3		5	6			14	8¹		11¹	12		7	4¹	9											1	10¹		
15	A	Raith Rovers	6-0		2	3¹		5	6	12		14¹	8		11¹			7	4¹	9²											1	10		
May 5	H	Motherwell	0-2		2	3	4	5	6			14	8		11	12		7		9											1	10		
7	A	Dundee United	1-0		2	3		5	6			8	14		12	11¹		7	4	9	16										1			
10	A	Hearts	1-3					6			8	9	3		11	10		5	14	16¹			12	2					1			4		7
TOTAL FULL APPEARANCES				26	32	22	27	18	29	19	23	13	34	4	6	24	24	14	10	7	7	6	5	4	7	4	1		1		1			1
TOTAL SUB APPEARANCES					1			1		6	3	12	1	16	4	5	9	5		3	2		11	6	11	5		3	1			1	1	
TOTAL GOALS SCORED							4	5		1		13	10	10		9	1	2	1	1			1					1						1

FINAL TABLE

	P	W	L	D	F	A	Pts
RANGERS	**36**	**25**	**6**	**5**	**85**	**33**	**80**
Celtic	36	23	7	6	78	33	75
Dundee Utd	36	17	10	9	47	33	60
Hearts	36	14	12	10	46	43	52
Dunfermline	36	12	15	9	52	65	45
Aberdeen	36	10	12	14	45	54	44
Kilmarnock	36	11	19	6	41	61	39
Motherwell	36	9	16	11	44	55	38
Hibs	36	9	16	11	38	55	38
Raith Rovers	36	6	23	7	29	73	25

THE AUTHOR

IAIN KING is the Chief Sports Writer of Scotland's best-selling paper, the *Sunday Mail*.
A winner of the Napier College medal for Journalism and the TS Murray Award for Scotland's top young reporter, he graduated to national news-papers from spells at the *Lanark Gazette* and a stint as sports editor of the *Ardrossan and Saltcoats Herald*.
Writing about football proved a better bet than playing after he was freed by juniors Thorniewood United and, after four years at the *Scottish Sun*, he moved to the *Sunday Mail*. At the age of 30, Iain has already been to 15 countries covering matches involving the Old Firm and Scotland.
He lives in his native East Kilbride with journalist wife Lorna and children Caitlin and Bruce.

ACKNOWLEDGMENTS

The launch of '9' came just six days after the team kicked their last ball of the season, an incredible achievement. That happened because of the huge amount of work from a very dedicated crew of people at First Press. I'd like to thank Steve Sampson for having faith in me at the start and Brian McSweeney, Neil, Robert and the gang for all their stunning design work. The patient library staff at the *Daily Record* and *Sunday Mail* also deserve a mention for all their help. I'd also like to thank Rangers Football Club, including chairman David Murray, manager Walter Smith and all the players past and present for their unstinting co-operation. I hope they like the end result.
Last but not least my boss George Cheyne, my dad Matt – a cold-eyed critic when I'd finished every chapter – and my long-suffering wife Lorna, who became a single-parent family during the writing of this book.

Designed, edited, published and distributed by First Press Publishing.

193/197 Bath Street, Glasgow, G2 4HU
Telephone: 0141 226 2200. Fax: 0141 248 1099

Author: IAIN KING
Production Editor: BRIAN McSWEENEY
Production Manager: HELEN WALSH
Sub-editor: TOM HUNTER
Graphics and design: ROBERT CHAMBERS & NEIL SHAND
Advertising Manager: KAREN SMYTHE (Tel: 0141 572 0572)
Distribution & Marketing Manager: RITA NIMMO